FINLAND

Christmas

TRAVEL GUIDE 2024

Experience Winter Magic in the Land of the Northern Lights — Must-See Destinations and Cultural Highlights

CURZIO MANNA

Copyright © 2024 by Curzio Manna

All rights reserved

No part of this publication may be reproduced, distributed, or transmitted in any form or by any means, including photocopying, recording, or other electronic or mechanical methods, without the prior written permission of the publisher, except in the case of brief quotations embodied in critical reviews and certain other noncommercial uses permitted by copyright law.

Disclaimer:

As the world evolves, so do the places you visit. Hotels may change ownership or close, restaurants may alter their menus or prices, museums may adjust their hours, and transportation options may shift. These changes may occur even after we have thoroughly researched these locations for you.

While we strive to keep everything as accurate and up-to-date as possible, certain details may change before the next edition. We kindly ask for your understanding if you notice any differences. Please note that we cannot be held liable for any inaccuracies, omissions, or inconveniences, as well as any resulting loss, damage, or expenses from the information provided.

We appreciate you choosing our guide and hope it helps you have a wonderful journey!

TABLE OF CONTENTS

INTRODUCTION — 13

Welcome to Christmas in Finland — 13

Best Time to Visit Finland for Christmas Festivities — 21

THE CHRISTMAS CAPITAL – ROVANIEMI — 31

Discovering the Official Hometown of Santa Claus — 32

Ranua Wildlife Park — 40

Arctic Circle and Crossing It — 43

Unique Experiences in Rovaniemi — 44

Best Accommodations in Rovaniemi — 48

FINNISH LAPLAND: A CHRISTMAS DREAMLAND — 57

Kittilä — 57

Inari — 62

Muonio — 63

HELSINKI - CHRISTMAS CHARM IN THE CAPITAL — 67

Unwrapping Christmas Markets in Helsinki 68

Traditional Finnish Christmas Dishes to Try in Helsinki 71

Helsinki Cathedral and Its Role in Christmas Celebrations 72

Shopping for unique Christmas gifts in Helsinki 72

Christmas Performances and Concerts 74

TURKU – FINLAND'S CHRISTMAS CITY 77

The Old Great Square Christmas Market 77

Turku Cathedral 80

Christmas Eve Traditions in Turku: 81

Best Places to Stay in Turku for a Cozy Christmas 84

TAMPERE – A WINTER WONDERLAND OF LIGHTS 87

Tallipiha Stable Yards 87

Tampere Christmas Market 88

Näsinneula Tower 90

Visiting the Moomin Museum 92

SAVONLINNA: A WINTER CASTLE WONDERLAND — 95

Olavinlinna Castle — 95

Savonlinna Christmas Market — 99

NORTHERN LIGHTS AND ARCTIC ADVENTURES — 103

Best Places to See the Northern Lights at Christmas — 103

Northern Lights Tours — 108

Kemi's SnowCastle — 110

Saariselkä — 111

BEYOND THE ARCTIC – CHRISTMAS IN THE FINNISH ARCHIPELAGO — 115

Åland Island — 116

Exploring the Coastal Cities — 117

FAMILY-FRIENDLY CHRISTMAS ACTIVITIES — 125

Ice Fishing and Building Snow Castles — 125

Visiting Elf Schools in Levi and Rovaniemi — 128

MoominWorld   131

PRACTICAL TRAVEL TIPS   **135**

Essential Tips for Winter Travel in Finland   135

Visa Requirements and Entry Information   143

Customs and Border Protection for Visitors   147

Health and Safety Concerns   148

LOCAL ETIQUETTE & CULTURAL TIPS FOR CHRISTMAS   **151**

Finnish Christmas Customs and Holiday Etiquette   151

Sauna Traditions at Christmas   153

Dos and Don'ts for Tourists during Finnish Winter Holidays   155

Respecting Sami Traditions in Lapland   157

UNIQUE FINNISH CHRISTMAS FOODS AND DRINKS   **161**

Must-Try Finnish Christmas Dishes   162

Christmas Buffets and Traditional Holiday Meals   166

Best Restaurants and Cafés to Try Finnish Holiday Cuisine
168

CHRISTMAS ITINERARIES IN FINLAND 173

3-Day Christmas Itinerary (Lapland Focus) 173

5-Day Christmas Itinerary (Helsinki and Lapland Combo)
176

7-Day Christmas Itinerary in Finland (Complete Holiday Experience) 181

FREQUENTLY ASKED QUESTIONS ABOUT CELEBRATING CHRISTMAS IN FINLAND 187

CONCLUSION 193

9 | Finland Christmas Travel Guide

11 | Finland Christmas Travel Guide

INTRODUCTION

Welcome to Christmas in Finland

Finland is a country with breathtaking natural beauty, mystical northern lights, and deeply ingrained cultural traditions. It is also often regarded as the ideal Christmas destination. From Rovaniemi, a miraculously placed village officially designated as Santa Claus' homeland, to an ancient Finnish tradition requiring a declaration of peace on Christmas Eve, Christmas in Finland is a magical spell that entertains both young and old. Whether exploring the calm beauty of snow-covered Lapland or visiting lively Christmas markets in historic cities like Helsinki and Turku, Christmas in Finland feels like entering a winter wonderland.

This guide will walk you through endearing Christmas customs in Finland, offer practical suggestions for first-time visitors, and explain why this Nordic treasure has become synonymous with Christmas magic.

Overview of Finnish Christmas Traditions

Finnish Christmas celebrations are rich in tradition, with the majority combining ancient pagan rites with Christian practices. Christmas holidays are primarily observed from early December until the 26th of December, including Christmas Eve, Christmas Day, and Boxing Day. However, one thing remains constant throughout the season: the comforting warmth of Finnish hospitality interwoven with the peacefulness of the frozen environment.

1. The Advent Season and Christmas Countdown

Christmas in Finland does not occur on the 24th or 25th; it begins much earlier. The Advent season, which lasts four Sundays before Christmas, is a time of anticipation and preparation for Christmas. Finnish families often burn a set number of candles for each Sunday of Advent, while children open Advent calendars stocked with chocolates and little gifts.

Traditional ornaments include himmeli and straw stars; Christmas trees, typically spruce or pine, are carried indoors on Christmas Eve or earlier, depending on preference, and adorned with handcrafted ornaments, candles, and tinsel.

2. The Christmas Sauna Tradition

Christmas sauna is a highly treasured tradition in Finland. On Christmas Eve, generally, in the early afternoon before the festivities begin, the family gathers and enjoys a sauna. This has been done for hundreds of years to symbolize the purification of the body and soul before the holiday.

For Finns, the sauna is a place to relax and reflect, and it takes on new meaning on Christmas Eve. According to legend, on this evening, the souls of deceased ancestors visit the sauna, imbuing it with a mysterious aura. It is a quiet time before the loud evening festivities.

3. Christmas Eve

Christmas Eve, of course, is the highlight of the holiday season in Finland. Around this time, people meet with their families for a festive supper that typically includes rosolli, a traditional beetroot salad; lanttulaatikko, or rutabaga casserole; and a main course that may be oven-baked ham or a sort of Christmas fish known as Joulukala. Glögi, a spiced mulled wine served warm with raisins and almonds as garnish, is frequently served alongside the meal.

After supper, Finnish families receive gifts, which are thought to have been carried in by Joulupukki, the Finnish equivalent of Father Christmas. Unlike the Western story of Father Christmas entering homes via the chimney, Joulupukki knocks on the front door, usually carrying a sack of presents. It is not uncommon for a family member to dress up as Father Christmas, much to the joy of the youngsters.

4. Declaration of Christmas Peace

Every Christmas Eve, a solemn and centuries-old custom is carried out in Turku, Finland's ancient capital. At noon, the Declaration of Christmas Peace is solemnly and ceremoniously read out on the balcony of Brinkkala House, signaling the official start of the Christmas season. For the first time, it dates from the 13th century and exhorts people to keep a holy holiday of peace with good joy, as well as to be polite during the festive season.

The declaration of reading is broadcast throughout the country, and many Finns tune in to watch or listen to the occasion, which represents a break from the daily grind, ushering in a calm, reflective Christmas season.

5. Christmas Day and Beyond

While Christmas Eve is the highlight, Christmas Day in Finland is a day of relaxation and spending time with loved ones. The Finns normally spend the mornings going to church, and the rest of the day enjoying the calm of the season. Tapaninpäivä, the day after Christmas, is also known as Boxing Day in Finland, and it is celebrated outdoors with activities such as sleigh rides, skiing, and snowshoeing.

Why is Finland the Ultimate Christmas Destination

The Christmas vision includes snow-covered landscapes, reindeer, and Santa Claus. Finland brings these imaginations to life, providing a unique Christmas experience. From the distant wilderness of Finnish Lapland to the vibrant Helsinki, from snug cottages to shining Helsinki streets, Finland is a place where Christmas enchantment is more than a dream; it is a way of life.

1. Rovaniemi: The Official Hometown of Santa Claus

Perhaps one of the most appealing aspects of visiting Finland during the Christmas season is the opportunity to visit Rovaniemi, which is said to be Santa Claus' official hometown. Rovaniemi, located in Finnish Lapland's Arctic Circle, exudes Christmas spirit all year. Santa Claus Village is a year-round Christmas wonderland with workshops, reindeer, and an actual Santa Claus post office that receives and answers letters from children all over the world.

Don't forget about Santa Park, which is only a short drive from Santa Claus Village. This site offers tourists interactive experiences such as Elf School, cookie crafting with Mrs. Claus, and underground ice galleries.

2. Northern Lights

Few natural phenomena are as visually stunning as the Northern Lights and Finland's Arctic is one of the best sites in the world to witness them. During the long, dark winter nights, the aurora borealis creates an extraordinary Christmas ambiance by pulsing the sky with bright green, purple, and pink colors.

Many resorts, like Saariselkä and Levi, offer guided excursions of the Northern Lights via snowmobile, reindeer sleigh, or husky sled. If this is too much, tourists can enjoy the light displays from glass igloos or Aurora cottages, where they can lie in bed and watch the lights dance over the sky.

3. Lapland: The Ultimate Winter Wonderland

In essence, Lappland is a Christmas dreamland. Imagine being pushed along on a sled by reindeer through snow-covered forests, racing across frozen lakes with the impetus of a speeding snowmobile, or silently mushing a husky sled into the wilderness. Winter adventures abound in Lapland, and Christmas itself appears to be a magical timescape from which stories almost write themselves.

Another unique experience to consider on a trip to Lapland is staying in an ice hotel. To that end, Kemi's SnowCastle is designed to provide guests with rooms covered in snow and ice, replete with snow sculptures and ice furnishings. This is a very unique bucket-list experience that elevates winter magic to new heights.

4. Christmas Markets and Festivities

Christmas markets in Finnish cities, particularly Helsinki and Turku, are among the nicest in Europe. Helsinki's Christmas Market, located on Senate Square, features over 100 vendors selling anything from handcrafted crafts to holiday decorations and local foods. There's also an old-fashioned merry-go-round for kids and plenty of warm glögi for everyone.

Turku, Finland's official Christmas city, hosts the historic Old Great Square Christmas Market, which adds medieval flavor to the festivities. Along with shopping for artisan goods and performances, visitors can sample traditional

Finnish Christmas sweets such as piparkakkuja, a type of gingerbread biscuit, and lipeäkala, dried cod.

5. The Unique Experience of a Finnish Christmas Sauna

Saunas can be found throughout the world, but the Finnish Christmas sauna is unique. When it's deep winter outside, nothing beats huddling in the heat of a sauna. During the Christmas season, however, the sauna takes on an even more symbolic role: it serves as a place of physical and spiritual cleaning for families preparing for the holidays.

First-Time Visitors Tips:

Christmas in Finland is an unforgettable experience; yet, a visitor must be prepared for the dangers that come with visiting a country during the cold months. Here are a few recommendations to help you plan the perfect trip to Finland:

Pack for Cold: In December, Finland may be quite cold, particularly in Lapland, where temperatures can reach -30°C (-22°F). Make sure you have adequate thermal layers on top of the insulated jacket to keep you warm. Wool socks and waterproof boots are ideal for dealing with the cold. There will also be a good pair of gloves and a cap to cover your ears.

Plan for Limited Daylight: Winter in Finnish Lapland means only a few brief hours of daylight at the winter solstice. On the bright side, the long evenings provide great conditions for stargazing with clear views and, if lucky, the Northern Lights.

Respect Local Customs: Most Finns are reserved, and making excessive noise in public is considered unpleasant. Furthermore, local 'house customs' require visitors to remove their shoes when entering a Finnish home.

Enjoy the Silence: The silence is probably the most spectacular aspect of Christmas in Finland. Snowscapes offer a quiet natural beauty that is both calming and rejuvenating. Give in to it, and you'll find a sense of calm that's hard to find anyplace else.

Best Time to Visit Finland for Christmas Festivities

Finland transforms into a winter wonderland from late November to early January, and this is the ideal time of year for anything Christmas-related. However, from early

December to the first week of January, Finland is truly at its most magical at Christmas. Also, the majority of Christmas festivities, winter sports, and opportunities to see the Northern Lights will be at their peak at this time.

Late November to Early December: The actual Christmas season begins at the end of November when Christmas markets open their stalls and lights in towns such as Helsinki, Turku, and Rovaniemi. This is when Lapland receives its first snowfall, and Rovaniemi's Santa Claus Village goes into overdrive. For those who dislike crowds but appreciate the festive spirit, this is an ideal time to visit.

Mid-December to Christmas Week: Christmas is in full swing, especially in Rovaniemi, Santa Claus' hometown. Events and activities abound, including reindeer sleigh rides, Christmas performances, and shopping at Christmas markets. If you've always wanted to experience a traditional Finnish Christmas, complete with Santa visits and a white Christmas, now is the time to go.

Christmas and New Year's Week: Many families visit Finland during this time to celebrate Christmas with traditional Finnish customs. It focuses on Christmas Eve (December 24), although it also includes Christmas Day and New Year's Eve. Expect large crowds, particularly in

Lapland and Helsinki, as well as a bustling celebratory atmosphere.

Early January: The first week of January is also ideal for anyone seeking a quiet, post-Christmas break. Although the Christmas decorations have begun to come down, the snow remains immaculate, and winter sports such as skiing, husky sledding, and Northern Lights hunting are in full force. Furthermore, Finland's winter landscapes remain breathtakingly magnificent well into the New Year.

Winter Weather: Preparing for Cold

Winter in Finland is lovely, but it is unquestionably cold, especially in the far north. It would be quite different depending on where one was going: southern Finland is significantly milder, whereas northern Finland's winter, which includes Lapland, is harsh.

1. Weather in Southern Finland (Helsinki, Turku)

In December, southern towns such as Helsinki and Turku may see temperatures as low as -3°C to -10°C (26°F-14°F). While not as snow-covered as Lapland in northern Finland, these towns are frequently lightly powdered by mid-

December, with a festive touch of snow in the middle of the winter.

While it is not as cold as the north, the wind combined with dampness from the Baltic Sea makes southern Finland feel rather cool, therefore suitable clothing is required. This lovely environment is created by regularly falling snowflakes, most of which are light, especially in locations with Christmas markets.

2. Weather in Northern Finland-Lapland, Rovaniemi

Temperatures in Finnish Lapland, where true winter magic unfolds, can reach extremely low levels, averaging between -10°C and -30°C (14°F to -22°F) between December and January. The Arctic region of Lapland is notorious for significant snowfall, with a thick layer of snow covering woods, lakes, and hills throughout the season.

It is a dry cold here, so it does not feel as hard as the wet cold in Southern Finland, but preparation is required to properly enjoy winter activities. This location also has periods of minimal daylight (and, in some cases, no daylight at all during polar night), which is perfect for viewing the Northern Lights.

3. How to Dress for the Finnish Winter

Layering is the key to survival and surviving in Finland's harsh winter. Here's a quick overview of what you should wear:

Base Layer: Begin with moisture-wicking thermal underwear (top and bottom). It is recommended to choose Merino wool or synthetic textiles since they retain heat and keep sweat away from your skin.

Middle Layer: A good fleece or wool sweater and thermal tights are recommended. These layers can trap heat and protect your body from the cold.

Outer layer: A high-quality, insulated, waterproof jacket and snow leggings are required. Make sure they are wind-resistant; the wind can cause a significant temperature difference.

Accessories:

- A thermal cap that covers your ears.

- **Gloves:** Choosing a glove that is both warm and waterproof is a smart idea. Mittens may be warmer than gloves in extremely cold weather.

- **Scarf or neck gaiter:** This protects your neck and face from really cold winds.

- **Wool socks:** Thermal or wool socks will keep your feet toasty. Waterproof boots have robust bottoms that prevent slipping on snow and ice.

Footwear: Wear insulated, waterproof winter boots with good traction in ice weather. Make sure your boots are large enough to accommodate thick socks but not too tight that they cut off your blood circulation.

4. Be Prepared for Limited Daylight

Winter in Finland is distinguished by its restricted daylight, which in Lapland is barely above the horizon for a few hours per day, if not at all, during polar night. In December, there will be approximately 6 hours of daylight in the south of Finland, while the extreme north will be virtually completely dark.

That should not deter you, however. The mellow hours of twilight cast a wonderful, almost mystical glow. Furthermore, many activities, including husky safaris, reindeer rides, and Northern Lights tours, are intended for low-light circumstances. Many sites were well-lit with festive lights, candles, and bonfires, making it feel less dreary even when it was dark.

Northern Lights and Snow: Planning Your Winter Wonderland

Only a few natural phenomena elicit as much awe as the Northern Lights, often known scientifically as the Aurora Borealis. Finland is one of the few areas in the world where it may be observed. Now, add Finland's unrivaled, snow-covered terrain to the mix, and you've created a winter wonderland right before your eyes. Here's how you may organize your trip around these magical ingredients.

1. Best time to see the Northern Lights

The Northern Lights are visible in Finland from the end of September to April, with December and January being the best months: the nights are long and dark, providing the perfect backdrop for this phenomenon. While the aurora can be seen as far south as Finland, heading north to

Lapland increases the chances of a successful seeing significantly.

Best Places to View:

Rovaniemi: Despite its popularity as a Christmas destination, it is also a fantastic spot to see the Northern Lights, however, you may need to venture outside of town to avoid light pollution.

- **Saariselkä:** Further north, this Saariselkä provides even better chances of seeing auroras. It is less popular than Rovaniemi and offers a more isolated experience.

- **Levi:** Home of ski resorts, Levi also offers great Northern Lights tours and lodgings, including glass igloos for aurora-watching from the comfort of your bed.

- **Kemi and Kittilä** are other good sites to look for auroras.

2. Planning Your Northern Lights Experience

Many guided trips take visitors on Northern Lights expeditions, usually by snowmobile, reindeer sleigh, or husky sled. Other resorts include Aurora Domes or glass igloos where you may enjoy the lights from the comfort of your accommodation.

Seeing the Northern Lights requires a great deal of patience and flexibility. The weather must be exactly right, and even then, sightings are not assured. Nonetheless, the best time to see one is between 9 p.m. and 2 a.m., when the sky is bright and the aurora is usually at its most visible.

3. Enjoying Finland's Winter Wonderland

Finland's white backdrop is not only breathtaking, but it also provides a limitless number of alternatives for winter sports:

Skiing and Snowboarding: The most popular alpine skiing and snowboarding resorts are Levi and Saariselkä. Both feature numerous slopes of varying difficulty levels. Cross-country skiing is also quite popular and one of the best ways to see Finland's vast snowy landscapes.

Husky and Reindeer Sledding: A traditional means of transportation is to ride across the cold wilderness on a reindeer-pulled sleigh or a husky sled. Similarly unique, they provide a fascinating opportunity to experience Lapland's breathtaking scenery.

Ice Fishing and Snowshoeing: If the severe sports listed above are too demanding for you, try ice fishing on a frozen lake or snowshoeing through Finland's pristine environment. Both activities allow you to reconnect with nature while enjoying the peace of winter.

If this Christmas holiday in Finland is perfectly planned, it will be one of those unforgettable experiences due to tradition, adventure, and natural beauty. From the Northern Lights in Lapland to family celebrations in Santa Claus' official hometown to quiet moments in Lapland's beautiful environment, Finland promises a magical Christmas season to remember.

THE CHRISTMAS CAPITAL – ROVANIEMI

Rovaniemi, generally known as Santa Claus' hometown, is the most enchanting and attractive of all Christmas destinations. Rovaniemi, in the heart of Finnish Lapland, is a year-round Christmas attraction. This is a destination for families, couples, and solo visitors looking to experience the enchantment of the holiday season, learn about Lapland's traditional culture, and appreciate the unique beauty of the Arctic Circle winter.

Rovaniemi has something for everyone, from children who want to meet Santa Claus to people who want to experience the magic of Christmas. The Christmas trip in this town is excellent, from Santa Claus Village to Santa Park, with a mix of cheerful festivals, amusing winter activities, and the breathtaking beauty of the Lappish countryside.

Discovering the Official Hometown of Santa Claus

Rovaniemi is widely recognized as Santa Claus' hometown. Since the middle of the twentieth century, this Lappish village has proudly identified itself as the Christmas gateway. Every year, millions of people travel to Rovaniemi to fulfill a childhood dream: visit Santa in person and explore a magical realm of seasonal traditions. But, more than that, Rovaniemi is not just a tourist trap; it has the true sense of Christmas--a location where people may rediscover a little Christmas joy and magic.

What to Expect:

- **Santa Claus:** Of course, Santa Claus is the main attraction. Meeting him in Rovaniemi is undoubtedly one of the most pleasant experiences for both children and adults--he is a kind, joyful, and inviting man who takes the time to listen to everyone's holiday wishes.

- **Year-Round Christmas:** In Rovaniemi, Christmas is celebrated all year, not just in December. Whether it's a snowy winter or a brilliant summer, Santa Claus Village is open all year to give tourists a sneak peek inside the wonderful tour.

- **Arctic Circle:** This essential line marks the southernmost point where you can see the midnight sun and polar darkness. When you cross the border, you will be in the Arctic. This adds charm to Christmas.

Santa Claus Village

It is located around 8 kilometers from the town of Rovaniemi. Santa Claus Village is the perfect place to celebrate Christmas. This world-famous attraction brings together everything you love about Christmas: snow-covered landscapes, festive decorations, and, of course, Santa himself.

Santa Claus' Village has something for everyone, whether they are traveling with children or simply want to relive their childhood delight. Here are some highlights you should not miss:

1. Meet Santa Claus in his office

One of the most appealing aspects of Santa Claus Village is the opportunity to meet the big man himself. For such circumstances, Santa's Office is open year-round, allowing visitors to take a seat with Santa and share their Christmas wishes regardless of the season. The encounter is intimate and personal, and regardless of age, it feels like a wonderful time.

Meanwhile, his workplace is decorated with Christmas ornaments and a plethora of toys, giving the impression of being in Wonderland. You might even have your photo professionally taken to keep the memory forever. Indeed, the magic of visiting Santa in Rovaniemi is not easily forgotten; for many guests, it was the highlight of their entire trip.

2. Santa Claus' Post Office

Another must-see attraction in the Village is Santa Claus' Main Post Office, where hundreds of letters from children all over the world arrive every day for Father Christmas. The post office elves analyze the letters to ensure that each one reaches Santa. Visitors can send their own Christmas cards and letters, with a special Arctic Circle postmark that will be retained by the postman who receives them.

The post office is a lovely room filled with colorful envelopes, drawings, and heartfelt messages to Santa. You can spend some time reading the letters and learning more about how Santa responds to mail from all over the world. It's a charming reminder of the world's devotion to Christmas and the character of Santa Claus.

3. Crossing the Arctic Circle

The Santa Claus Village allows visitors to cross the Arctic Circle, a geographically and symbolically significant frontier. Crossing the Arctic Circle is an important milestone for many tourists, and it is commemorated here with Christmas magic.

The Arctic Circle is demarcated by a conspicuous white line across the Village, allowing tourists to easily cross and enter the Arctic. You can even obtain a certificate proving that you have crossed this boundary.

Santa Park

Santa Park, located not far from Santa Claus Village, is another must-see site. Unlike the open-air village, this is an underground theme park located within a man-made cave. An immersive experience that makes you feel like you've walked into Santa's enchanted wonderland.

Santa Park offers a variety of activities and views that bring the Christmas imagination to life. The following are some of the highlights:

1. The Elves' Workshop

The Elves' workshop is one of Santa Park's magical attractions, where both children and adults may observe the busy elves at Santa's service. The elves are busy preparing for Christmas by constructing toys, wrapping presents, and spreading joy.

The visiting guests join in the excitement, assisting the elves with their responsibilities, such as learning to wrap presents or creating traditional Finnish Christmas pastries. The workshop is filled with laughter and excitement, and the wonderful smell of holiday delicacies is one of the most memorable aspects of each visit.

2. The Ice Princess Castle

A trip to Santa Park isn't complete without exploring the fantastic world of the Ice Princess. Her ice castle is stunning, with glistening walls and glittering lights reminiscent of a winter wonderland.

The Ice Princess welcomes her guests with grace and charisma, showing them around her ice castle. There is even an ice slide available for children and adults to enjoy, making the location both exciting and interactive. The Ice Princess frequently performs, and her theatrics enhance the experience for both youngsters and adults.

3. Gingerbread Bakery

Prepare to roll up your sleeves at Santa Park's Gingerbread Bakery, where guests may decorate traditional Finnish gingerbread creations. With a little help from the bakery's merry elves, basic gingerbread cookies are transformed into culinary pieces of art.

This project is especially enjoyable for children, who like getting creative with frosting and sprinkles. Plus, you get to take your masterpieces home--if you can avoid eating them first.

4. Elf School

Visitors at Elf School can learn how to be jolly from Santa's elves. It's a fun exercise that teaches you how to be an honorary elf, including the traditional skill of manufacturing toys, wrapping gifts, and spreading festive cheer.

Graduates of the Elf School get a diploma, providing a fun and interactive way to delve further into the wonderful world of Santa's little helpers.

5. Magic Train

Experience the Magic Train, which promises indoor excitement around Santa Park's hidden nooks and crannies. The train travels through a variety of wonderful locales, including glimpses of Santa's toy factory, elves' quarters, and other scenes of Christmas festivities. It is soft and lovely, and it could be a good choice for families with little children who like spotting all the Christmas touches.

Winter Fun beyond Christmas Magic

While Santa Claus Village and Santa Park promise a world of Christmas pleasure, Rovaniemi offers a variety of winter-themed activities. Here's what you can do in Lapland's winter splendor, from thrilling outdoor activities to cozy nights by the fire:

1. Reindeer and Husky Safaris

A reindeer or husky safari is an essential part of every Lapland visit. Meet Santa's reindeer in person in Rovaniemi and take an incredible sleigh ride through the snow-covered forest, learning about how the local Sámi people have used these creatures for millennia. Alternatively, experience the thrill of being towed by a pack of enthusiastic huskies as you fly across the Arctic wilderness in your sled.

2. Northern Lights Tours

Rovaniemi is one of the best spots in the world to witness this stunning natural light show, in which brilliant colors decorate the night sky. Guided excursions transport visitors outside of town to get the best views of this wonder. You will see the aurora in ideal conditions if it is visible at all.

3. Snowmobiling

Snowmobiling is an enjoyable winter pastime in Rovaniemi for those who require a little more speed. Snowmobile across the frozen wilderness to experience the breathtaking

Lappish environment, from frozen lakes to snow-capped mountains.

4. Ice Fishing and snowshoeing

You can even attempt ice fishing on a frozen lake or go snowshoeing in the peaceful Arctic environment. Both activities provide an opportunity to calm down, breathe in the crisp winter air, and appreciate the Lappish environment.

Ranua Wildlife Park

Ranua Wildlife Park is a must-see for any animal enthusiast or adventurer visiting Rovaniemi. This park is roughly an hour's drive from Rovaniemi and provides a unique opportunity to observe Arctic species in their native snow habitats. Ranua Wildlife Park is open all year, but it becomes even more magical during the winter months when the entire park is completely covered in snow and ice.

Ranua is home to over 50 types of northern and Arctic creatures, some of which would be unbelievable to see in the wild. These majestic creatures against the backdrop of Lapland's winter scenery are truly beautiful. Here is what to expect when visiting this wildlife park.

1. Meet the Arctic Animals

One of the most fascinating aspects of visiting Ranua Wildlife Park is the opportunity to observe a variety of Arctic species that most people have never seen. You'll be able to see such animals up close while trekking along its snowy trails.

- **Polar bears** are one of the most iconic animals in the Arctic, and the park is well-known for them. Seeing these massive, muscular beasts moving across the snow is awe-inspiring.

- **Wolves and lynxes** are extremely elusive predators that are difficult to see in the wild; at Ranua, you may view them in their native habitat.

- **Reindeer and Moose:** It's impossible to visit Lapland without seeing reindeer, and Ranua Wildlife Park is an ideal place to see them in their cold surroundings, as well as moose, the woodland giant.

- **Owls, Arctic Foxes, and Eagles:** The park also boasts a variety of bird species, ranging from snowy owls to golden eagles, and you may encounter adorable yet robust Arctic foxes.

2. Winter Safari & Animal Encounters

Ranua Wildlife Park provides guided tours and safaris that allow you to explore the park's winter habitat. Enjoy a winter drive-through safari through snow-covered landscapes, observing animals' active behavior and learning how they adapt to life in the Arctic. You might even get to participate in feeding sessions and witness how each one interacts with its surroundings.

3. Fun Family Amusement

Ranua Wildlife Park is ideal for families with children. The park has a children's zoo where children can meet and even play with smaller animals like goats and bunnies, as well as numerous winter picnic areas. After exploring the park, youngsters can play on an ice playground.

4. Ranua End

Combine this with a memorable overnight stay at Ranua Wildlife Park Resort, which offers charming cabin-style accommodations directly near the park. Imagine waking up to the sound of wolves howling or spending a tranquil winter night in a glass-roofed igloo while the Northern Lights dance over you.

Arctic Circle and Crossing It

Crossing the Arctic Circle is one of the most memorable parts of any trip to Rovaniemi. This crossing, an invisible line circling the globe at latitude 66°33' north, marks not just a geographical landmark but also the Arctic, the ultimate marker of adventure for many explorers.

Rovaniemi features the literally and symbolically evident Arctic Circle, which should not be missed if you're out for some fun; here's what awaits you as you officially "cross the line":

1. The Arctic Circle Line at Santa Claus Village

The most well-known line for crossing the Arctic Circle is located in Santa Claus Village, where visitors can walk across it. The line physically runs through the center of the settlement, and crossing it formally marks entry into the Arctic zone. It is a moment that is frequently documented with photographs; you can even obtain an official certificate certifying that you have crossed the Arctic Circle.

Many visitors see crossing the Arctic Circle as a meaningful milestone. It serves as a sort of affirmation that you have arrived in one of the world's least crowded and most singularly individualistic regions.

2. What Does It Mean to Cross the Arctic Circle?

The Arctic Circle marks the boundaries of an area where the sun does not rise in the winter or set in the summer. These two phenomena are known as polar night and midnight sun. Crossing the Arctic Circle during the winter brings you into a zone of tremendous seasonal contrasts, with short days and lengthy winter nights illuminated by the Northern Lights.

3. Crossing Mark

Most travelers pass at Santa Claus Village, where they can purchase Arctic-themed souvenirs to commemorate their journey. In addition to the certificate of crossing, each guest can be photographed with the "Arctic Circle" marking.

Unique Experiences in Rovaniemi

Rovaniemi offers a variety of unique experiences in addition to the traditional winter activities. Rovaniemi has something for everyone's interests, from adrenaline rushes to calm times to soak up the enchantment of Lapland. Here are some of the most unique activities you shouldn't miss.

1. Chasing the Northern Lights

The Northern Lights are the most popular attraction in Rovaniemi. The Northern Lights are a natural phenomenon that appears on clear nights during the months of September through March. The colors green, pink, and purple churn into a stunning spectacle across the night sky.

There are numerous ways to see the Northern Lights in the Rovaniemi area:

- **Northern Lights Safaris:** These tours take you out of town to dark, secluded regions, giving you a much better chance of seeing the aurora. You can go by snowmobile, husky sled, or even reindeer sleigh to add an extra degree of adventure to your search for the Northern Lights.

- **Crystal Igloos and Aurora Bubble:** A superior category includes not only daytime activities but also sleeping in a glass-roof igloo or an Aurora Bubble-- lie in bed and watch the aurora dance above you in the warmth and comfort of your private cabin.

2. The Arktikum Science Museum

A visit to the Arktikum Science Museum is a must for everyone interested in learning more about the Arctic region. This museum is fascinating with its exhibits on the natural environment, history, and culture of the Arctic and northern Finland. You can learn about the indigenous Sámi people, experience Arctic animals, and observe how life has evolved in this harsh climate.

Another highlight of the museum is the glass tunnel that provides a wonderful view of the snow outdoors. If you're planning a winter trip, this is a great spot to warm up and learn more about the region.

3. Sámi Culture and Reindeer Encounters

Be astounded by the customs and history developed by the indigenous Sámi people, who have lived in northern Scandinavia for hundreds of years. Among other things, you can visit Sámi reindeer farms in Rovaniemi, learn about their centuries-old ways of life, and take part in traditional celebrations. A reindeer sleigh ride is an enlightening and very natural way to explore the forest, led by Sámi guides who share their knowledge of the area.

4. Husky Sledding

Husky sledding is an adrenaline junkie's method to explore the Arctic tundra. Husky safaris, which take you through snowy forests and frozen lakes with a team of enthusiastic huskies, range from short introductory rides to multi-day expeditions where you may learn to operate your sled.

5. Snow and Ice Experiences

Rovaniemi is well-known for its snow and ice sculptures; every winter, artists from all over the world travel there to create fascinating ice constructions and snow castles. Even if you don't stay there, you can explore one of the region's ice hotels, which have everything from the walls to the furnishings made of ice. You can drink something at an ice bar.

6. Ice Swimming and Sauna

Ice swimming followed by a hot sauna is the quintessential Finnish experience. This is one of the most stimulating local practices for improving circulation and lowering stress levels. Several lakes in the region have created ice-swimming zones, allowing visitors to take brief dips in frigid water before immediately warming up in a nearby sauna.

Best Accommodations in Rovaniemi

Rovaniemi accommodations range in price and style to appeal to travelers of all budgets. Here's a rundown of where you can stay during Christmas, whether it's a fancy hotel, a cottage, or somewhere more affordable.

Luxury Accommodations

People who want to spend their time in Rovaniemi in the most comfortable and memorable way should look at a variety of luxury hotels. They provide breathtaking views, first-rate service, and one-of-a-kind Arctic experiences.

Arctic TreeHouse Hotel

- **Overview:** This historic hotel offers guests charming wooden suites set amid the treetops, complete with panoramic windows that provide views of the surrounding forest and the Northern Lights from all directions.

- Special touches include elegant décor, private saunas in select rooms, and the ability to enjoy the aurora from the comfort of your bed.

- **Budget:** During the high season, prices start at about € 450 per night.

Santa's Igloos Arctic Circle

- **Overview:** This modern glass igloo, located in Santa Claus Village, is ideal for viewing the Northern Lights and the Arctic sky. Each igloo features a private bathroom and modern amenities.

- Glass roofs for viewing the aurora, as well as proximity to Santa Claus Village activities, distinguish this property.

- **Budget:** Approximately € 300-€ 450 per night.

Arctic Light Hotel

- **Overview:** The Arctic Light Hotel is a modern boutique hotel in the heart of Rovaniemi. This modern design lodging combines a modern decor with a cozy atmosphere. Each room at the Arctic Light Hotel is uniquely furnished, making it suitable for style-conscious tourists.

- This upscale boutique hotel features an on-site gourmet restaurant and elegant, uniquely furnished rooms.

- **Budget:** €300-€500 per night.

Mid-range Accommodations

If you wish to strike a balance between comfort and budget, these mid-range lodgings provide a good selection of services, amenities, and unique experiences.

Lapland Hotels Sky Ounasvaara

- **Overview:** This hotel is located on the Ounasvaara fell and is equipped with modern entertainment facilities; it provides easy access to winter activities such as skiing and snowboarding. It also offers spectacular views of the Arctic environment.

- **Special Features:** Rooftop sauna, easy access to outdoor activities.

- **Budget:** €150-€300 per night

Snowman World Glass Resort

- **Overview:** This resort in Santa Claus Village offers magnificent glass cottages with outdoor hot tubs, making it ideal for couples or families looking for a unique stay in a modern Arctic setting.

- **Unique Feature:** Floor-to-ceiling windows allow you to see the aurora, and there are outdoor private hot tubs.

- **Budget:** €300-€400 per night.

Budget Accommodations

Those on a tighter budget will discover a variety of comfortable, convenient places to stay in Rovaniemi that do not sacrifice location or amenities.

Hostel Cafe Koti

- **Overview:** Hostel Café Koti, located in the city center, offers everything from individual rooms to shared dormitories in a clean, modern setting. It is an excellent choice for budget guests who want to be within walking distance of the city's major attractions.

- **Unique Features:** Luminous Scandinavian style and on-site café.

- **Budget:** Dormitory beds start at €50 per night and private rooms at €120 per night.

Guesthouse Borealis

- **Overview:** A family-run guesthouse near the station in a quiet area with basic but comfortable accommodations. It is a wonderful low-cost choice for budget-conscious travelers who wish to see Rovaniemi without spending money on lodgings.

- **Unique features** include a homey ambiance, a peaceful environment, and a low price.

- **Budget:** €70 to €100 each night.

Santa's Hotel Rudolf

- **Overview:** This budget-class hotel is centrally located in the city and offers a variety of basic but sufficiently maintained rooms. It lacks frills, yet it is conveniently located near the majority of Rovaniemi's stores and eateries.

- **Unique features**: Because the resort is within walking distance, the rates are lower than at other nearby resorts.

- **Budget:** €70-€120 per night.

Unique and Alternative Accommodations

Those looking for a one-of-a-kind experience will appreciate these unusual lodgings that showcase the Arctic's majesty.

Glass Resort

- **Overview:** Glass Resort, located in Santa Claus Village, provides modern glass apartments with amenities such as private hot tubs and saunas. Ideal for guests who wish to experience the splendor of the Arctic while being surrounded by luxury.

- **Unique features:** The glass walls and ceilings offer stunning views of the starry sky and the Northern Lights.

- **Budget:** Approximately €400-€700 per night, depending on season and suite style.

Ounasvaaran Lakituvat Chalets

- **Overview:** These chalets are positioned immediately near the ski resort of Ounasvaara, providing both exciting and peaceful experiences. Each hut has a sauna and a fireplace for added comfort after a day in the snow.

- **Unique features:** It is situated near the ski slopes, making it excellent for winter activities.

- **Budget:** €150-€250 per night.

Villa Arctica

- **Overview:** This property is in a quiet setting just outside of the city. It has three bedrooms, a sauna, and all the amenities of a home. Ideal for families or small groups in need of personal privacy.

- **Unique Features:** Fully equipped kitchen, sauna, and stunning views of the surrounding forest.

- **Budget:** €200-€300 per night.

Conclusion

A Christmas vacation in Rovaniemi is more than simply a getaway; it is a fantastic voyage to a place where the spirit of Christmas lives all year. From the very crucial tete-a-tete with Father Christmas to the fascinating underground world of Santa Park, from the stunningly beautiful views of the Northern Lights to spotting arctic creatures in Ranua Wildlife Park, every moment spent in Rovaniemi is magical. This naturally gorgeous country is rich in legacy and offers an amalgamation of incredibly exciting winter sports and rich cultural heritage under one roof, making it the ideal Christmas vacation for travelers of all ages.

FINNISH LAPLAND: A CHRISTMAS DREAMLAND

Finnish Lapland can be considered a Christmas wonderland. Finnish Lapland is known for its pure wildness, sparkling snow scenery, and unique holiday experiences. From the tiny hamlet of Kittilä to the crowded slopes of Levi Ski Resort, the deeply cultural Sami customs of Inari, and the unspoiled landscape of Muonio, this is truly a Christmas wonderland that offers both adventure and cultural experiences.

In this section, we take a look at some of the top attractions in Finnish Lapland, from Kittilä and Levi to Inari and Muonio. Lapland has something for everyone's taste, whether you're an adventurer looking for thrills, a family looking for festive fun, or a culture enthusiast interested in learning about historical traditions.

Kittilä

Kittilä, located in the heart of Finnish Lapland, is a charming village surrounded by snowy fells and breathtaking wildlife. Aside from being a picturesque hamlet, the most well-known destination, the Levi Ski Resort, is only 15 minutes away. Levi is one of Finland's largest ski resorts, which makes it quite popular during the winter season, particularly around Christmas.

Levi Ski Resort

Levi Ski Resort provides first-rate amenities for both winter sports lovers and families. Levi caters to everyone's demands, from first-timers who want to try skiing or snowboarding for the first time to seasoned sportsmen looking for a thrill.

- **Slopes-Skiing and Snowboarding:** This resort's ski slopes are designed for skiers of all skill levels, from beginner to experienced. Families can enjoy easy slopes to their hearts' content, while more difficult routes provide a solid challenge for advanced skiers and snowboarders. Levi is even recognized for its FIS Alpine World Cup slalom events, where visitors may watch top skiers compete.

- **Night skiing** is one of the many thrilling activities to do in Levi, particularly under floodlights. Skiing in the dark is a thrilling and bizarre experience due to the long Arctic evenings in the winter.

- **Christmas Events and Festivities:** During December, Levi is transformed into a Christmas wonderland. Meeting Santa Claus, Christmas markets, and live entertainment have all been scheduled. Levi is a magical spot to celebrate the holiday season, with horse-drawn sleigh rides, Christmas carol singing, and a variety of other activities for youngsters.

Aside from skiing and Christmas-related events, Levi has plenty of room for relaxation: from après-ski lounges and spas to restaurants that welcome families with children and scenery alike, Levi has all you need for a memorable Christmas break.

Reindeer Farms and Traditional Lappish Cuisine

Certain aspects of Lapland are iconic, and a visit to this significant region would be incomplete without a stop at one of the numerous reindeer farms. Many such farms dot the countryside around Levi, providing insight into the Lapps' culture and traditions.

- **Reindeer Sleigh Rides:** The most traditional activity in Lapland, reindeer sleigh rides will transport you through snow forests with only the sound of hooves on snow. Most farms offer guided tours during which visitors can learn about reindeer herding customs that have been passed down for centuries.

- **Reindeer Farm Visits:** In addition to sleigh rides, tourists can meet, feed, and hear tales from local herders about the importance of reindeer in Lappish culture.

Traditional Lappish cuisine is another feature of a visit to Reindeer Farms or Levi. Lappish cuisine is hearty and flavorful, made with locally sourced resources including reindeer, wild berries, and fish from neighboring rivers. Poronkäristys (reindeer stew) and lohikeitto (cream salmon soup) are two traditional Lapland meals that should not be missed. Most Levi's restaurants combine classic dishes with modern additions to produce something unique.

Levi Ice Hotel

Spending the night at the Levi Ice Hotel is a totally unique experience. This hotel, built completely of ice and snow, provides a fantastic overnight stay in rooms that resemble frozen pieces of art. Each year, the hotel is renovated, and the rooms are decorated with exquisite ice sculptures and shimmering ice furnishings.

- **Ice Rooms:** With a fur-lined, heated bed and an insulated sleeping bag, the sub-zero temperature is surprisingly comfortable. The hotel's interior stays about -5°C, with ice walls and furniture creating a fantasy world.

- **Dining & Bars:** The hotel also has an ice bar where beverages are served in ice-filled glasses, as well as a snow restaurant that serves warm meals in a pleasant and cozy setting. Having dinner or lunch with ice all around is a bizarre experience that will be remembered for years to come.

- **Activities around the Hotel:** Guests staying at the Levi Ice Hotel may participate in activities such as an ice sculpture workshop, snowshoeing, and Northern Lights excursions. Seeing the Northern Lights while staying in a hotel built of snow and ice is a once-in-a-lifetime experience.

Inari

Inari, located further inland in Finnish Lapland, is arguably the hub of Sami culture. The Sami people, who are indigenous to the Arctic, and have their own elaborate Christmas traditions that are deeply rooted in nature and habits accumulated over the ages.

Visiting Traditional Sami Villages and Markets

A visit to Inari allows you to see and experience traditional Sami settlements. During Christmas, these communities come alive with Sami marketplaces selling handicrafts, various types of jewelry, and clothing.

Duodji refers to traditional Sami handicrafts manufactured mostly from natural materials such as reindeer hide, birchwood, and antlers. From Christmas markets, you may buy everything from pensively made swords to intricately woven linens, each a reminder of the Sami people's strong connection to their environment.

Sami Christmas Traditions and Cultural Experiences

Inari is also an excellent spot to experience Sami Christmas celebrations: the Sami people have traditional Christmas music, dances, and storytelling, so visitors will gain an understanding of this distinct culture.

Joik singing is one of the most moving aspects of Sami culture; it is an ancient kind of singing that is strongly tied to the land, animals, and the spirit realm. Special joiks are performed during the Christmas season, creating a hauntingly lovely mood.

Other excursions included seeing traditional reindeer herding in Inari. Reindeer herding is a very traditional occupation that has persisted to this day and is still extremely important in the life of the Sami people; tourists are invited to learn about the role of reindeer in Sami culture, particularly around Christmas.

Muonio

Muonio is a great place for visitors seeking the quiet beauty of the Arctic tundra. Muonio, located near Pallas-Yllästunturi National Park, provides a site for any outdoor enthusiast looking to spend Christmas in the most stunning natural splendor of Lapland.

Snowshoeing and Hiking Through Frozen Forests

Snowshoes provide a fantastic view of the Muonio environment when it is covered in snow. Snowshoeing allows you to travel deep into the snow and reach regions that are inaccessible during the winter.

- **Guided Snowshoe Tours:** With a local guide, you will travel through frozen forests and across the tops of fells, learning about the distinctive local flora and animals along the route. You may even see some wildlife, such as reindeer and polar foxes while learning about how arctic animals live in such extreme conditions.

- **Hiking in the Stillness of Winter:** One of the many distinguishing characteristics of Muonio hiking is the Arctic Wild's great silence. The snow absorbs sound, creating an otherworldly quiet that is both peaceful and uplifting.

Cross Country Skiing at Pallas-Yllästunturi National Park

Cross-country skiing is a popular activity in Lapland, and Pallas-Yllästunturi National Park has some of the best ski tracks in the country. The park has nearly 500 kilometers of groomed paths that weave through forests, overfalls, and along frozen lakes.

The trails are built for all skill levels, from novice to advanced skiers. From a relaxing glide through snow-covered woodlands to a vigorous excursion across the open fells, the park has something for everyone.

Aside from skiing, on clear nights, breathtaking views of the Northern Lights can be viewed, adding a whimsical touch to this cross-country ski vacation.

Conclusion

During the Christmas season, Finnish Lapland transforms into a separate realm. Outdoor exhilarating adventures, intriguing cultural traditions, and pristine natural beauty combine to make every aspect of Lapland a magical Christmas destination. Every stop, from the slopes of Levi Ski Resort to the Sami reindeer herding traditions in Inari to the undisturbed Arctic nature of Muonio, provides a distinct experience. From skiing down snow-covered fells to a reindeer sleigh ride or resting in an ice hotel, Finnish Lapland offers an extraordinary Christmas break full of wonder and adventure.

HELSINKI - CHRISTMAS CHARM IN THE CAPITAL

Helsinki in December is like opening a greeting card: it's an invitation to a city shrouded in the lovely air of winter, where small Christmas markets and all the lights blend with the unique Nordic magical touch. If you're planning a trip to Finland around the holidays, Helsinki has a lot to offer: from traditional Christmas markets to gourmet holiday feasts, it's one destination that will be unforgettable for travelers trying to get in the holiday spirit.

Unwrapping Christmas Markets in Helsinki

As December approaches, the streets of Helsinki take on a Christmas-like atmosphere, with Christmas markets being the most notable examples. These locations bring locals and visitors together in a friendly setting typified by warm lights, handicrafts, and the aroma of spiced dishes that permeate the air.

Helsinki Christmas Market

The Helsinki Christmas Market at Senate Square is one of the best places to visit during the holidays. This Christmas market exemplifies a wonderful blend of Finnish tradition and festiveness, with over 100 stalls selling anything from locally crafted crafts to holiday treats.

Crafts and Goods:

- Beautiful Pottery

- Wool Scarves

- Leather Goods

- Traditional Finnish woodworking

Seasonal Delights

- Glögi-mulled wine.

- Piparkakut - gingerbread cookies

- Karjalanpiirakka and Karelian pies

Furthermore, the Christmas ambiance on Senate Square, combined with the architectural background of Helsinki Cathedral, elevates this market to one of the most stunning Christmas destinations.

Senate Square

This square is the crown jewel of Helsinki's festive scene, home to the city's most recognizable holiday adornment, the Giant Christmas Tree. Every year, a lovely tree is chosen from the forests of Finland. When this enormous tree is lit, it radiates festive magic throughout the square.

Nighttime Beauty:

- Twinkling lights against the snow-covered ground.

- Grand neoclassical architecture paired with lively decorations

Senate Square is a must-see location throughout the holiday season, whether for a leisurely evening stroll or to capture the ideal photo in front of the tree.

The Esplanadi

Take a wonderful winter walk down The Esplanadi, a popular Helsinki district known lovingly as "Espa" by locals. During the holidays, the Esplanadi will transform into a lovely avenue lined with trees adorned with shimmering lights, charming stores, and cafes.

Ambiance:

- When it snows, the scenery is lush and lovely.

- Cozy cafes provide blankets and heaters for outdoor dining.

After some window shopping, stop by one of the many cafes for a nice drink and watch the world go by.

Traditional Finnish Christmas Dishes to Try in Helsinki

Finnish food takes center stage during this time of year, and if you happen to be in Helsinki, you're in for a special treat. Local restaurants and cafes serve a variety of traditional cuisines that are hearty, comforting, and perfect for a cold winter day.

Joulukinkko-bre Burnt Christmas Ham

- Glazed with Mustard

- Served with side dishes such as lanttulaatikko or swede casserole and perunalaatikko or potato casserole.

Graavilohi pickled fish (cured salmon)

- Generally served on rye bread with mustard sauce.

Riisipuuro ("rice porridge"):

- Creamy dessert served with cinnamon and sugar.

Many Helsinki restaurants offer special Christmas menus during December, so make sure to try as many of these festive meals as possible while you're there!

Helsinki Cathedral and Its Role in Christmas Celebrations

Standing boldly over Senate Square, Helsinki Cathedral is one of the most identifiable structures in town, and it occupies a special place in people's minds during the Christmas season.

During the holiday season, the cathedral also hosts Christmas Day services and concerts, so whether you want to attend the mass or simply enjoy the beautiful views of the illuminated cathedral at night, this is a memorable element of the Christmas enchantment in Helsinki.

Shopping for unique Christmas gifts in Helsinki

Helsinki's Christmas shoppers can find almost anything. Stock up on high-quality Finnish design goods or more traditional mementos, and visit the city's many stores and marketplaces.

Stockmann Holiday Window Display

Once the holidays arrive, one of the city's most beloved traditions is the opening of the Stockmann Christmas window show. This prominent department shop takes up all the stops, constructing a spectacle so wonderfully detailed that people travel from miles away to see it.

Attraction:

- Fantastic scenes, captivating for both young and elderly.

After you've been amazed at the show, Stockmann's vast assortment of products has something for everyone, whether you're looking for Finnish design, fashion, or Christmas decorations.

Finnish Design and Handicrafts at Local Boutiques

Helsinki's Design District is a dream come true for individuals looking for high-end Finnish design.

Notable Brands

- **Iittala** is known for its gorgeous glassware.

- **Marimekko:** Famous for bright and vibrant designs.

Smaller businesses provide handcrafted jewelry, ceramics, and other crafts that embody the Finnish aesthetic: clean, basic, and nature-inspired.

Traditional Souvenirs:

- Mittens knitted by hand

- Saami-inspired leather products.

- Woodcarvings

These will make wonderful gifts or memories to remember your time in Finland.

Christmas Performances and Concerts

Music is an important component of Helsinki's Christmas celebrations, and there are several opportunities to hear choir performances, classical concerts, and holiday carols during your visit.

Attending Christmas Mass in Finnish Churches

In addition to the services at Helsinki Cathedral, the majority of the city's churches host Christmas masses and other special holiday events.

Experience:

- Beautiful way of understanding the underlying meaning of Christmas.

- Often accompanied by moving choral music

Temppeliaukio Church, sometimes known as the Rock Church, is one of the oddest music settings. The acoustics inside the church, which is hollowed out of solid rock, are extraordinary, and the ambiance is especially wonderful during the Christmas season.

Christmas Choruses and Classics

Throughout December, there are various Christmas concerts in Helsinki, many of which feature the Helsinki Philharmonic Orchestra or resident choirs.

Venues:

- Finlandia Hall

- St. John's Church

These performances offer a beautiful way to listen to seasonal music and are a perfect accompaniment to the festive events taking place across town.

The handcrafted gifts, Christmas music in the old church, and, most importantly, downtown Helsinki with all of its lights make for a wonderfully comfortable, charming Christmas. It is ideal for everyone who wants to celebrate Christmas in the Nordic style.

TURKU – FINLAND'S CHRISTMAS CITY

Turku, Finland's oldest city and an officially designated Christmas city, provides a one-of-a-kind experience during this time of year, combining history, traditional ambiance, and festive charm. This wonderful city is preparing to dress up like a Christmas fairy tale town every year, with its enticing marketplaces, historic performances, and age-old customs, attracting visitors from all across Finland and other countries.

The Old Great Square Christmas Market

The Old Great Square Christmas Market is the focal point of all seasonal activities in Turku. This market nearly seems to come alive with its magical ambiance amidst its historic surroundings and the glow of twinkling lights, and it will be a must-see for anybody experiencing the city this Christmas season.

Traditional Market Stalls

- Featuring local handicrafts and crafts.

- Wooden toys, handmade ornaments, wool scarves, and other distinctive Finnish presents.

Seasonal Delights

- Glögi-warm

- Freshly baked piparkakut

- Traditional Finnish Christmas sweets

This market is more than simply a shopping destination; it's also a gathering spot for both locals and visitors to enjoy the festive atmosphere.

Medieval Markets and Artisan Products

Turku Christmas markets incorporate elements of theme shops and a dash of medieval flare to enhance the shopping experience. Some of the items you can see at these Christmas markets are:

Artisan Goods:

- Blacksmiths practicing traditional business, hand forging tools and ornaments.

- Leather artisans create unusual wallets and belts.

- Pottery, ceramics, and woven textiles

- Custom jewelry created from natural stones and metals.

These medieval markets provide visitors with a look into Turku's rich past while also providing a completely unique shopping experience.

Seasonal Performances and Historic Shows

Throughout the Christmas season, many historical shows and seasonal performances retrace Turku's history. Many performances are held around the Old Great Square and Turku Castle to add to the city's enchanting aura at this time of year.

Re-enactments:

- Historic plays with medieval costumes and plots;

- Musicians and choirs dressed in their traditional clothing.

Theater Performances:

- All local theaters in Turku will have Christmas-themed plays, as well as open-air theatrical performances including caroling and storytelling.

These activities ignite the Christmas mood and immerse visitors in Turku's festive customs.

Turku Cathedral

The Declaration of Christmas Peace, held every year on Christmas Eve in front of the Turku Cathedral, is one of Turku's most popular Christmas traditions.

Significance:

- It is one of the oldest Christmas customs, dating back to the 13th century and originating in Finland.

- It's the start of Christmas in Finland.

Atmosphere:

- Thousands of people assemble around the cathedral.

- Following the solemn statement, Christmas carols are sung.

This tradition is widely televised throughout Finland and is an integral feature of Turku's Christmas celebration.

Christmas Eve Traditions in Turku:

Christmas Eve afternoons in Turku are filled with stately traditions and joyful customs. Following the Declaration of Christmas Peace, the majority of Turku families spend the day together and participate in various traditions.

Christmas Sauna:

- A Finnish tradition in which families relax and spend quality time together before feasting at Christmas.

Decorating the Tree:

- Some of the ornaments on Finnish Christmas trees are handmade from wood, while others are constructed of candles and straw.

Lighting Candles in the Cemetery:

- Many families visit cemeteries and put candles around the graves of their loved ones, creating a serene but poignant scene.

Dining on Traditional Finnish Christmas Meals

Food is particularly important during Christmas in Turku, and during the season, eateries in the city serve some of the most distinctive Finnish Christmas delicacies. Do not miss out on the following.

Joulukinkku, or Christmas Ham:

- A succulent ham is frequently coated with mustard and served alongside side dishes like swede casserole and potato casserole.

Rosolli (Finnish Christmas salad):

- A bright beetroot salad usually served with a creamy dressing.

Kalapöytä (Fish Table):

- A variety of cured fish, such as graavilohi (cured salmon) and silli (pickled herring).

These dishes embody the essence of Finnish cuisine and provide tourists with an authentic flavor of Christmas in Finland.

Outdoor Ice Skating and Bonfires

In addition to its numerous markets and culinary delights, Turku offers a plethora of winter activities to add to the festive atmosphere. For starters, ice skating is the most popular holiday activity, and outdoor skating rinks can be found all throughout town.

Ice Skating Rinks:

- Rinks are set up in public parks and squares, usually surrounded by kiosks selling hot drinks and snacks.

- Visitors can hire skates and join the locals.

Bonfires:

- In some regions of the city, large bonfires are constructed to keep people warm and also serve as a gathering spot for family and friends.

- Other regions provide mulled wine and sausages that can be roasted over an open fire.

In this way, it produces a pleasant community-oriented setting ideal for getting into the holiday spirit.

Best Places to Stay in Turku for a Cozy Christmas

Turku has a wide range of accommodations to suit any taste, from low-budget to more upscale.

Luxury Options:

- The **Radisson Blu Marina Palace Hotel** provides rooms with views of the Aura River, and modern conveniences, **and is close to Christmas markets.**

- **Hotel Kakola:** A boutique hotel in a former prison that offers one-of-a-kind stays in luxurious comfort and style.

Mid-Range Options:

- **Scandic Julia** is a central hotel that is ideal for families; it adds to the festive atmosphere and provides easy access to all Christmas attractions. Centro Hotel Turku: recognized for its warm greeting and cozy accommodations, the hotel will make your winter break even more comfortable. Budget options:

- **Omena Hotel Turku** is a low-profile, low-budget hotel that provides budget guests with comfort and convenience.

- **Linnasmäki Hostel:** a little cheaper, in a quieter area, with common kitchen facilities where you can self-cater if you choose.

Whatever one's taste for staying, Turku's hospitality and nostalgia for a holiday are unforgettable.

Conclusion

Turku has earned the title of Finland's Christmas City thanks to its historical traditions, magnificent marketplaces, and pleasant activities. Turku's historically rich setting, along with cultural customs and holiday spirit, has something for everyone, from announcing Christmas peace to cozy bonfires and legendary dinners.

The city has something unique to offer its visitors, whether it's a random stroll through the ancient marketplaces or the Christmas Eve liturgy at Turku Cathedral. When you visit during the holiday season, you will be enveloped in a joyous, heartwarming atmosphere that truly reflects the essence of Finnish Christmas.

TAMPERE – A WINTER WONDERLAND OF LIGHTS

Tampere, Finland's third-largest city, combines metropolitan attractiveness with captivating Christmas customs. Tampere transforms into a winter wonderland during the holidays, complete with dazzling lights, bustling Christmas markets, and family-friendly attractions. Tampere has something for everyone, whether you want to explore its historical streets or enjoy festive dining.

Tallipiha Stable Yards

Tallipiha Stable Yards are one of the most gorgeous sites in Tampere during the Christmas season, combining history with festive cheer. This was once part of the Finlayson cotton mill estate; now it serves as a picturesque backdrop for one of Tampere's most popular Christmas markets.

Atmosphere:

- The lights, Christmas trees, and general illumination are all decorated in a charming, old-world setting with classic wooden structures, adding to the nostalgic feel of the holiday.

Market Stalls:

- Local craftsmen sell handicrafts such as woolen items, ceramics, and wooden toys.

- Handmade candles, jewelry, and holiday decorations

- Locals sell traditional Finnish sweets including glögi (mulled wine) and piparkakut (gingerbread biscuits).

Horse Carriages:

- Horse-drawn carriage rides throughout the vicinity of the Christmas Market are possible to enhance the magic of these ancient surroundings.

- Tallipiha is a must-see destination for visitors looking for a genuine Finnish Christmas Market.

Tampere Christmas Market

Tampere Christmas Market is one of the city's most popular winter attractions, and it is conveniently located in the city center. During the event, both locals and visitors gather in

Central Square to celebrate the festive season with enchantment in the air.

Wooden Stalls:

- Over 100 wooden kiosks selling handcrafted Finnish items and seasonal specialties.

- Traditional Finnish handicrafts include hand-knitted socks, leather goods, and reindeer-themed things.

Food and Drink:

- A variety of local cuisine includes savory Karjalanpiirakka, sausages, and lohikeitto (salmon soup).

- Heating gluhwein with glögi and other traditional Finnish Christmas drinks

- Sweet treats, like joulutorttu (Christmas tarts with plum jam)

Events:

- Live music and carolers add to the festive atmosphere.

- Special visits from Santa Claus for families with children.

- Ice sculptures and light displays that add to the festive atmosphere.

The Tampere Christmas Market is a great place to buy and relax in a festive setting.

Näsinneula Tower

The renowned Näsinneula Tower is perhaps the best place in Tampere to have a Christmas meal with a view. As a 168-meter-high observation tower, it provides spectacular panoramic views of Tampere and the surrounding lakes, which are especially stunning in the winter when the landscape is completely white.

Dining Experience:

- Näsinneula, located at the top of the restaurant, offers superb dining with a spinning view of the city.

- Guests can order a special Christmas menu with Finnish delicacies such as smoked salmon with dill, reindeer filet with lingonberry sauce, traditional Christmas casseroles, and Finnish sweets.

Views:

- As one dines, the restaurant revolves, providing a 360-degree panorama of the winter wonderland below.

- The bright Christmas lights in Tampere combine with the snow-covered environment to produce a magnificent spectacle.

Näsinneula Tower is ideal for anyone looking to combine fantastic meals with beautiful views over the holiday season.

Visiting the Moomin Museum

Tampere is unusual in that it is home to the world's only Moomin Museum, which serves as a family Christmas trip. The Moomins, created by author Tove Jansson, are among Finland's most beloved inventions and have become an integral part of Finnish culture. Visiting over Christmas adds a magical touch to the occasion.

Exhibitions:

- Visitors can explore original drawings, 3D scenes, and relics from the world of the Moomins.

- The museum has interactive exhibits that allow kids to engage with the stories in a playful way.

Christmas at the Museum:

- During the Christmas season, the museum decorates with Moomin-themed embellishments.

- Christmas workshops for kids in which children will make various Moomin crafts such as Moomin ornaments and cards.

- Storytelling during the Christmas season, when the Moomin Christmas tales are narrated.

Moomin Merchandise:

- The museum shop stocks a variety of Moomin Christmas items, including soft toys, books, and kitchenware.

A Christmas visit to the Moomin Museum is quite magical, and families with young children may immerse themselves in the intriguing world of the Moomins over the holidays.

Conclusion

Tampere blends dazzling lights, festive markets, and iconic landmarks, making it the ideal winter trip around Christmas. Everything is present in this winter wonderland, from the ancient charm of Tallipiha Stable Yards to the stunning view from Näsinneula Tower. Add in a spectacular trip to the Moomin Museum, and you've got a Christmas event that combines culture, tradition, and pleasure.

Whatever your heart desires, whether it's authentic Finnish crafts, excellent food, or the magic of the Moomins shared with your family, Tampere will ensure an amazing

Christmas. So cuddle up, grab a cup of glögi, and prepare to experience the enchantment and wonder of Tampere's holiday season.

SAVONLINNA: A WINTER CASTLE WONDERLAND

Savonlinna, located in the heart of Finland's Lakeland, is a magical Christmas destination with elements of medieval charm in its winter beauty. This area transforms into a winter wonderland with the famed Olavinlinna Castle, which towers high over the freezing waters of Lake Saimaa and provides historical and natural attractions in their most distinctive form during the Christmas season. From Christmas markets on the lake's banks to guided candlelit tours of an ancient fortress, this fantasy town has plenty for those looking to get into the Yuletide spirit.

Olavinlinna Castle

Olavinlinna Castle, which dates back to the 15th century as a medieval castle, is the centerpiece of Savonlinna's Christmas festivities. Olavinlinna, located on a small island in Lake Saimaa, is one of Northern Europe's best-preserved medieval fortresses. During the winter, this location will take on a new magic.

Christmas Decoration:

- During the holiday season, tastefully decorated lights, Christmas trees, and wreaths cast a warm and welcoming glow on massive stone walls.

- A massive Christmas tree stands in the courtyard, giving the ideal photo opportunity for guests to take home.

Medieval Atmosphere:

- Walking through the castle's historic halls is sure to put you in the mood for a medieval getaway.

- This distinguishes the castle, erected on the snow-covered island, and creates a fairytale-like environment that is particularly spectacular to experience during the Christmas season.

Special Events:

- Between early December and Christmas, the castle hosts medieval reenactments, live music, and storytelling sessions that bring Olavinlinna's history to life.

Candlelight Tours and Festive Reenactments

One of the most romantic ways to see Olavinlinna Castle during the holidays is to take one of its candlelight tours. Visitors take special guided tours by candlelight through the castle's magnificent halls and secret corridors to experience a fascinating environment that feels almost like stepping back in time.

Candlelight Exploration

- Flickering candlelight cast shadows on the castle's ancient stone walls, adding to the mystery of history in air and form as one navigates these dark hallways.

- Well-informed guides regale visitors with fascinating knowledge about the castle's medieval past, including legends of knights, kings, and battles that once raged within its walls.

Festive Reenactments:

- Festive medieval reenactments over the Christmas season contribute to this experience within the castle grounds.

- Actors dressed in classic medieval attire portray scenes from Christmas feasts and other courtly celebrations in the castle, providing an insight into what Christmas would have been like hundreds of years ago.

These tours and reenactments make Christmas at Olavinlinna Castle an engaging and memorable experience.

Winter Boat Cruises on Lake Saimaa

Despite the fact that Lake Saimaa's waters are partially frozen throughout the winter, a winter boat tour in Savonlinna allows you to observe Finland's largest lake. It entails discovering a unique way to explore the stunning Finnish Lakeland environment throughout your vacation.

Scenic Views:

- You will take a winter boat tour on the freezing waters of Lake Saimaa, with beautiful views of snow-covered islands, frozen coastline, and the towering Olavinlinna Castle, which stands majestically on its island.

- The placid beauty of the lake in winter, along with the crisp air and peacefulness, makes it very amazing.

On-board Comfort:

- The boats have heated cabins, allowing you to take in the spectacular sights while staying toasty.

- Some cruises offer hot drinks such as glögi and hot chocolate, as well as traditional Finnish pastries, to keep you warm throughout the ride.

Northern Lights

- And, if you're lucky, you might see dancing flashes of the Northern Lights across the sky while on this cruise. An extra layer of wonder for your Christmas adventure in Savonlinna.

Savonlinna Christmas Market

A holiday in Savonlinna would be incomplete without a visit to the Savonlinna Christmas Market. The following market, put up near the beaches of Lake Saimaa, allows visitors to feel the spirit of the festive season right in the heart of a lakeside setting.

Local Handicrafts and Souvenirs:

- There are several stalls selling handicrafts made by Finnish hands, such as traditional woolen clothes, reindeer hides, and wonderfully crafted ornamental items.

- Local artisans sell a variety of handicrafts, including wooden toys, hand-forged knives, and exquisite jewelry.

Food and Drinks:

- Savonlinna's Christmas Market is well-known for its wonderful seasonal delights, such as karjalanpiirakka (Karelian pasties), lohikeitto (creamy salmon soup), and freshly baked Christmas pastries.

- You can accomplish this by warming up with a cup of glögi, eating plates of cinnamon buns, or sampling some joulutorttu-Finnish Christmas tarts.

Lakeside Tradition:

- The fact that the market is located on the banks of frozen Lake Saimaa makes it distinctive and a must-see for those looking to purchase Christmas gifts or simply have a good time.

- Local choirs or musicians will occasionally perform seasonal melodies, contributing to the overall cheerful and warm environment.

Conclusion

Savonlinna provides something unique: the magic of Christmas as it would have been in medieval times, juxtaposed against the tranquility of nature. Whether it's taking candle-lit tours through old halls at Olavinlinna Castle, taking cruises across frigid Lake Saimaa, or simply enjoying the festive mood at the Savonlinna Christmas Market, this winter wonderland has something for everyone.

History aficionados will enjoy the festive reenactments and candlelight tours at Olavinlinna Castle, which transport people back to the Middle Ages. Nature enthusiasts will especially enjoy the winter boat rides, which offer breathtaking views of the frozen lake and surrounding scenery. For buyers looking for unique gifts, the Savonlinna Christmas Market offers a variety of local crafts and traditional Finnish cuisine set against the picturesque lakeside backdrop.

NORTHERN LIGHTS AND ARCTIC ADVENTURES

At Christmastime, Finland's Arctic nature transforms into a winter wonderland of natural beauty and adventure. For many people, visiting Finland during the winter is an opportunity to witness a natural wonder: the Northern Lights. However, this does not imply that Finland's Arctic area is only home to the Aurora Borealis. It is a site where adventurous excursions, such as snowmobile safaris, reindeer sleigh rides, and even stays in ice castles, provide an opportunity to visit unlike any other.

Here we look at some of the top Christmas destinations for the Northern Lights, as well as the unique Arctic experiences you can have in Rovaniemi, Levi, Saariselkä, and Kemi.

Best Places to See the Northern Lights at Christmas

The Northern Lights are a beautiful natural light display that illuminates the sky in greens, purples, and reds. This is caused by the collision of solar particles with the Earth's atmosphere, and the resulting spectacle is visible in high-latitude areas such as Finland. One of the main reasons tourists visit Finland during the winter is to observe the Northern Lights, and Christmas provides an excellent environment.

Rovaniemi

Rovaniemi, the capital of Finnish Lapland, is well-known and admired for being Santa Claus' official hometown. However, it is also a good site for viewing the Northern Lights. Because of its proximity to the Arctic Circle, the city sees Aurora regularly, particularly from October to March, when long evenings produce excellent circumstances for watching this phenomenon.

Northern Light Tours:

Rovaniemi offers a selection of Northern Lights trips designed to give you the best chance of seeing the Aurora Borealis. These cruises frequently combine Aurora searching with other Arctic excursions, including:

- **Reindeer Sleigh Rides:** Travel through the cold countryside on a genuine reindeer sleigh while looking for the Northern Lights.

- **Snowmobile Safaris:** Board a snowmobile and speed through dark, snowy places in search of the Aurora.

- **Aurora Domes:** If you prefer to remain comfortable while waiting for the lights, Aurora Domes offers heated, transparent igloos for unlimited views of the night sky from the comfort of your bed.

Levi

Levi is one of Finland's most famous ski resorts, located in the municipality of Kittilä in Finnish Lapland. Whereas skiing and snowboarding are popular here, Levi is an excellent area to watch the Northern Lights, thanks to its rural position and limited light pollution.

Aurora Sightings:

- Levi has among Finland's darkest skies, providing a clear glimpse of the Northern Lights on evenings with significant solar activity.

- The Levi Northern Lights Village is a unique location where you may stay in Aurora cottages with glass roofs and enjoy the Aurora from the comfort of your bed.

Aurora Hunting:

- Aside from such lavish Aurora cabin alternatives, Levi also provides a variety of Northern Lights experiences, including snowshoe adventures, snowmobile tours, and even huskie-led dog sled rides.

Saariselkä

Saariselkä in northern Finnish Lapland is a good hunting location for people seeking privacy and calm to observe the Aurora. Saariselkä, one of the most famous winter sceneries, is known for its high elevation, which increases the chances of seeing the Aurora.

Northern Lights Experiences

- It's ideal for big, open skies, and it's one of the few sites where you can see the Aurora while snowshoeing up a mountaintop or skiing along wilderness routes.

- There are also Aurora cabins and glass igloos in Saariselkä, which provide cozy and comfortable ways to view the Northern Lights.

Kemi

Kemi, located on the Gulf of Bothnia, may not be as well-known as the other destinations on this list, but it is an exciting option for Northern Lights hunters, particularly those who want to combine the Aurora experience with a stay at the incredible SnowCastle (more on that below). Although Kemi is further south than Rovaniemi and Saariselkä, it still has an excellent chance of witnessing the Northern Lights in December, January, and February, especially during peak solar activity.

Sea Ice Adventure:

- Kemi is unique in that it provides Northern Lights viewing from the frozen sea. To see the Northern Lights, join snowmobile rides or icebreaker cruises across the icy Gulf of Bothnia.

Northern Lights Tours

No trip to Finnish Lapland is complete without viewing the Northern Lights. These journeys are supposed to take you away from the artificial lights of towns and cities and into closer touch with nature in all her Arctic grandeur. Whether following the Aurora on a snowmobile, sleigh ride, or on foot, these trips provide some pretty adrenaline-fueled ways to experience the majesty of the Northern Lights.

Reindeer Sleigh Rides

A reindeer sleigh ride through snowy woodlands is one of the most traditional Finnish Christmas activities. Reindeer are a significant element of Lappish culture, and the calm, peaceful pace of a reindeer sleigh ride is ideal for enjoying the peace of the Arctic night while waiting for the Aurora.

Where to Go:

- Many sections of Lapland, including Rovaniemi, Levi, and Saariselka, offer reindeer sleigh rides.

- Most sleigh rides take approximately an hour, with some trips offering longer excursions that include a stop at a Lappish kota, a traditional Sami tent with hot drinks and nibbles beside the fire.

Snowmobile Safaris

If you're looking for a high-speed adventure, searching for the Northern Lights is both practical and enjoyable on snowmobile safaris. It travels over wider areas in shorter periods to increase the odds of seeing clear skies and possibly capturing the Aurora.

What to Expect:

- Snowmobile safaris often begin in the early evening, and after a little instruction on how to drive a snowmobile, you're off into the wilderness.

- Many excursions include pauses along the way where you may warm up by the fire, have a hot drink, and, if you're lucky, see the Northern Lights dancing overhead.

Aurora Domes

Aurora Domes offers the ultimate luxury experience for anyone looking to enhance their Northern Lights viewing.

These heated translucent igloos allow you to see Aurora from the comfort of your cozy bed.

Where to Stay:

- Aurora Domes can be found at several sites throughout Finnish Lapland, including Rovaniemi and Levi.

- Each one has a clear north wall or roof, which provides unhindered views of the sky.

Kemi's SnowCastle

One of the most unusual things you can do in Kemi is sleep in the world-famous SnowCastle. The SnowCastle, built on an ice and snow foundation, is an architectural marvel that transforms into a wonderful Christmas fairyland each year.

What to Expect:

- Every winter, the SnowCastle is rebuilt with a new design and, on occasion, theme. That's makes each visit unique.

- Inside, you'll find ice sculptures, snow-carved walls, and even ice beds, complete with thermal sleeping bags for warmth.

Dining at the Snow Castle:

- SnowRestaurant is unique; even the tables and chairs are made of ice. Dine on a traditional Finnish meal served on a dish of ice as the candlelight glow bounces off the ice walls surrounding you.

Northern Lights Viewing:

- Because of its distant location, SnowCastle is a wonderful place to see the Northern Lights. A few tourists go all the way and even spend the night in one of SnowCastle's icesuits, waking up the next morning to the potential of witnessing Aurora right outside their door.

Saariselkä

Saariselkä is located in northern Finnish Lapland and is Finland's northernmost ski resort. It attracts people seeking a Christmas escape from more remote places. The area around Saariselkä is peaceful, picturesque, and rich in snow-covered landscapes and untouched wilderness--one of the best places for Aurora hunting and winter sports.

Skiing and Snowboarding:

- Saariselkä, while not as huge as Levi's, offers excellent skiing and snowboarding options, particularly for novices and families. The resort has multiple slopes and cross-country skiing trails that wind through the surrounding wilderness.

Aurora Hunting:

- Saariselkä is one of the greatest spots in Finland to watch the Northern Lights because of its elevation and absence of light pollution. Aside from guided tours, many guests rent warm Aurora Cabins or glass igloos for a more intimate view of the nighttime display.

Snowy Cabins, Reindeer Safaris, and Aurora Hunting

You will discover the ideal base for your Arctic adventure in Finnish Lapland, with options ranging from icy cottages to Aurora-viewing accommodations. Staying in a cabin with snow-covered trees outside the window, and potentially witnessing the Northern Lights from there, is an important aspect of the Lappish Christmas tradition.

Reindeer Safaris:

- Reindeer safaris are available across Lapland, providing a calm, relaxing opportunity to explore the winter wilderness while learning about Sami culture and traditions.

Aurora Hunting Tours:

- Aurora hunting tours, whether by foot, sleigh, or snowmobile, are designed to enhance your chances of seeing the Northern Lights. Many excursions include breaks at lovely areas where you can relax with a nice drink by the fire while you wait for the lights to appear.

The Northern Lights and Arctic adventures are what make a Finnish Lapland Christmas very magical. From the thrill of a snowmobile pursuit to the serene peace of a reindeer sleigh ride, Finland's Arctic regions offer a limitless variety of activities. Whether in a cabin snuggled in the snow, a glass igloo, or even inside the Ice Palace itself, the natural beauty of the Arctic and its stunning light shows will leave an indelible impression.

BEYOND THE ARCTIC – CHRISTMAS IN THE FINNISH ARCHIPELAGO

While the Arctic north of Finland is known for its winter splendor, Christmas on the Finnish Archipelago is unique and equally enchanting. These islands and coastal cities along the country's coast are alive with festive customs that exude nautical charm and seasonal joy. Traditional Finnish customs, paired with winter ferry trips and attractive Christmas markets, characterize tourists to the Åland Islands and other coastal cities like Porvoo and Naantali, not to mention maritime gastronomic delicacies. This part will take you on an exciting Christmas trip to Finland's coastline.

Åland Island

The Åland Islands, located in the Baltic Sea between Sweden and Finland, offer a distinct Christmas celebration that blends Finnish and Swedish customs. This autonomous territory, famed for its stunning archipelago landscape, changes into a winter paradise at Christmas, complete with snow-capped islands, quaint town markets, and warmly lit homes.

Traditional Christmas Saunas:

- In Åland, the beloved Finnish tradition of Christmas sauna is given a unique maritime touch. Many locals and visitors enjoy a sauna by the sea, and the majority of them then take a refreshing plunge into freezing waters to restore their bodies and spirits in preparation for the holidays.

Festive Food:

- Åland boasts unique culinary traditions. Local delicacies on Christmas tables include thick rye bread (Åland bread), smoked herring, Christmas ham, and various pickled fish. During the holidays, indulge in glögg and Åland pancakes with stewed plums.

Winter Ferry Rides:

- A popular winter activity in the Åland Islands is the ferry journey across the freezing Baltic Sea. Ferries connecting Åland with mainland Finland and Sweden provide panoramic views of the ice archipelago. Wrap up warmly and stroll out onto the terrace to enjoy the beauty of snow-covered islands, which creates a serene and peaceful environment. Many boats are adorned for Christmas, and you can eat seasonal food and sweets onboard.

Exploring the Coastal Cities

Porvoo and Naantali, two seashore Finnish towns, offer a blend of historical allure and beach beauty to visitors. These picturesque old villages, with their lovely wooden buildings and meandering cobblestone pathways marvelously coated in snow, provide an unforgettable Christmas experience.

Porvoo - A Christmas Wonderland

Porvoo, located only 50 kilometers from Helsinki, is one of Finland's most ancient cities and is well worth a visit during the Christmas season. It has a very well-preserved Old Town with colorful wooden cottages that make it look like a storybook during the Christmas season.

Quaint Coastal Christmas Markets:

- The Porvoo Christmas Market, which takes place directly amid the Old Town, is a must-see for any traveler. The atmosphere is pleasant, with wooden stalls selling handicrafts and local artwork, as well as typical Christmas goodies like piparkakku (a type of gingerbread biscuit) and glögi (mulled wine).

Porvoo's Historic Street Tour:

- Walk from here to the Old Town, which is bordered by cobblestone streets and filled with tiny boutiques and galleries. Many of these shops sell Finnish design goods and handicrafts, making this an excellent place to browse for unique Christmas gifts.

Porvoo Cathedral:

- Notably, a Christmas visit to the Porvoo Cathedral is not to be missed. During the season, a 13th-century medieval church was beautifully lit and decorated. Its Christmas Eve ceremony, which includes all traditional Finnish hymns, can be emotionally moving.

Naantali

Naantali is another coastal jewel known for its quiet port, classic wooden buildings, and the surrounding Moominworld, a popular destination for families.

Christmas Market at the Sea:

- Naantali's Christmas market is located on the waterfront, and the snow-covered boats and frozen sea provide a picturesque setting. It sells handmade gifts, artisanal foods, and plenty of festive happiness. You may take a trip across the waterfront to observe the historic wooden buildings with their dazzling lights.

Naantali Church:

- The stunning Naantali Church is a stone church from the 15th century that provides a serene environment for Christmas celebrations. Visitors can join in on Naantali's Christmas services alongside the locals.

Winter Walks and Bonfires:

- Naantali's seaside walkways are ideal for winter walks. During the holiday season, bonfires are lit outside, and folks congregate around to warm themselves, sing Christmas songs, and sip hot beverages.

Coastal Christmas Dinner and Seafood Delicacies

The Finnish shore is well-known for its delicious seafood, which is especially popular during the holiday season. Åland, Porvoo, and Naantali offer memorable Christmas dinners featuring fresh fish from the Baltic Sea among traditional Finnish holiday foods.

Smoked and Pickled Fish:

- Most Finnish coastal Christmas feasts feature smoked and pickled fish, particularly herring and salmon. These will be served with rye bread and savory salads such as rosolli, which is a beetroot and potato salad.

Seafood Buffets:

- On Christmas, restaurants in these coastal cities frequently provide seafood buffets featuring fish, shrimp, and crayfish, among other delicacies. Buffets are arguably the greatest way to sample all sorts, which are frequently accompanied by schnapps or beer.

Traditional Finnish cuisine:

- Aside from shellfish, other typical Finnish Christmas meals include Joulukinkku, or Christmas ham, lanttulaatikko, or swede casserole, and karjalanpiirakka, or Karelian pasties, which are commonly served alongside seafood for a wonderful, complete holiday meal.

Holiday Treats:

- No Finnish Christmas lunch is complete without a variety of sweet delicacies. Make sure to taste Joulutorttu, a puff pastry filled with prune jam, and piparkakku, the traditional Finnish gingerbread biscuit. These pair perfectly with a nice cup of glögi, Finland's version of mulled wine infused with cloves, cinnamon, and cardamom.

Winter Ferry Rides and Snowy Island Exploration

Winter ferry rides are a popular component of any Finnish Christmas. The calm journey across the ice-cold Baltic Sea is tranquil enough. The archipelago's islands are covered in snow, resulting in an awe-inspiring winter seascape best seen from the deck of a ferry.

Ferry Rides to the Åland Islands:

- The Åland Islands boat offers stunning views of the snow-covered archipelago, making it a top winter adventure. Some of these boats offer Christmas cruises with festive cuisine, interesting programs, and, on occasion, Santa Claus to keep company.

Exploring the Snowy Islands:

- Once you get on the islands, you will have plenty of options to explore. The numerous tiny islands can be accessed on foot or with snowshoes, through snow-covered forests and along frozen coasts. Visit Åland's local museums and old churches, which are beautifully decorated during the holidays.

The Åland Islands are tranquil, while Porvoo and Naantali have their historical beauty. Finland's archipelago and coast weave together a Christmas that combines maritime customs with a joyous atmosphere. Whether it's seafood by the sea, Christmas markets in little villages, or a winter boat journey, the Finnish coast offers an appealing way to spend Christmas away from the Arctic.

FAMILY-FRIENDLY CHRISTMAS ACTIVITIES

Finland's stunning winter landscapes will present a plethora of activities ideal for children over the holiday season, like ice fishing on frozen lakes, making snow castles, visiting Elf Schools, and seeing the wonders of Moominworld. The nation is rich in activities that will keep both youngsters and adults entertained and fascinated. Whether your family is looking for magic in Santa's homeland or a winter adventure in one of Finland's coastal cities, these Christmas activities will provide excellent family bonding opportunities.

Ice Fishing and Building Snow Castles

Aside from such activities, ice fishing and constructing snow castles are popular winter hobbies, particularly for families looking to spend Christmas outside. These activities allow you to relax and be creative while experiencing Finland's amazing natural beauty.

Ice Fishing:

Finland's thousands of lakes and frozen waterways make it an ideal location for this type of sport, which Finns have practiced for centuries. Despite appearances, ice fishing is a strangely fascinating and family-friendly hobby if the families are patient and quiet enough.

Where to go Ice Fishing:

- During the Christmas season, most family-friendly resorts in Finland offer ice fishing, with Rovaniemi, Levi, and Saariselkä being among the most popular. Guided ice fishing tours are commonly available and typically include all equipment, such as ice augers, rods, and bait, as well as heated shelters to keep you warm while you wait for the big fish.

Experience:

- Ice fishing is especially popular among children, who enjoy the anticipation of waiting for a fish to nibble on the bait beneath the ice. A family can sit around a hole bored into the ice, swapping stories and warm beverages while waiting for a catch. The local guides frequently assist in teaching children the fundamentals, making the sport both enjoyable and educational.

The Catch:

With a little luck, many guides will even assist you in preparing and cooking the fish on-site. This adds to the thrill for the kids because they may enjoy the prize for their patience: cooking the fish over an open fire on the frozen lake.

Building Snow Castles: Creativity and Winter Fun

Making snow castles is a common family activity in Finland. With so much snow over the Christmas season, there is plenty of opportunity to create amazing snow sculptures that capture the imaginations of both children and adults.

Competitions at Snow Castle:

- Most regions in Finland, particularly Rovaniemi and Kemi, host snow castle-building competitions for families. These events encourage family creativity and teamwork as participants compete to build the most beautiful snow fortresses, complete with walls, turrets, and even snowmen to protect the entrance. Many of these competitions culminate with rewards for the best designs, which adds to the fun for the youngsters.

Build Your Snow Castle:

- For families that prefer a more casual snow vacation experience, simply venture out into the winter wonderland and have fun in the snow. Snowplay spaces are frequently given in accommodations, particularly in Lapland, where children may build castles, snowmen, and whatever else their imaginations can come up with.

Staying in a Snow Castle:

- The experience is elevated in Kemi by seeing the Kemi SnowCastle, an incredible ice and snow building that is rebuilt each year. It can also be a delightful pastime for families to explore frost-cut rooms, including sleeping in the ice hotel, which features snow beds, ice sculptures, and a restaurant serving warm meals in ice-cold settings.

Visiting Elf Schools in Levi and Rovaniemi

The Elf School provides a one-of-a-kind wonderful experience for children visiting Finland during the

Christmas season. With campuses in Rovaniemi and Levi, this school welcomes children inside Santa's realm, where they may learn elf skills and meet some of Santa's most important helpers.

Rovaniemi Elf School

In Rovaniemi, Santa's Official Hometown, children can enroll in Elf School, where they are taught the ways of an elf by Santa's trusted assistants.

What to Expect:

- Elf School takes children on a fantastic voyage to the North Pole, where they learn the mysteries of toy-making, gift wrapping, and even baking delicious gingerbread cookies--a prerequisite for any elf. The elf teachers also educate the children on how to communicate with the reindeer, sing elf songs, and perform the all-important Elf Dance. Each child receives an Elf Diploma at the conclusion, certifying them for a position in Santa's trusted workforce.

Meet Santa:

- No visit to Elf School is complete without meeting Santa Claus. Once the children have completed their training as young elves, they will be able to meet Santa in person, express their Christmas wishes with him, and take a tiny souvenir home with them.

Levi Elf School

Just around the corner from Levi, one of Finland's top ski resorts, is the Elf School, an outdoor-oriented version of the experience in which youngsters can learn all about the wonder of the Arctic while playing in the snow.

Activities at Levi Elf School:

- Levi's Winter Wonderland Elf School: The guiding elves teach children the secrets of reindeer herding, snow crafts, and winter wilderness navigation. Children's activities include building snow lamps, ice decorations, and even reindeer chow for Christmas Eve.

Family-Friendly Fun:

- Levi's Elf School is particularly popular with families due to its outdoor activities. In addition to elf training, the program offers snowshoeing, sledding, and even reindeer sleigh rides throughout the neighborhood. It all culminates with a lovely campfire gathering where the kids receive their Elf Certificates and hot chocolate with marshmallows.

MoominWorld

For families visiting Finland's southern coast, a Christmas visit to Moomin World in Naantali is simply amazing, bringing some of the beloved characters from the Moomin novels alive. Moomin World is an entertaining theme park featuring Tove Jansson's popular Moomin characters, which makes it particularly appealing to families with young children.

A Winter Wonderland in Moominworld

Moominworld, a traditional summer vacation, is turned into a winter paradise that will enchant both children and adults this Christmas.

Meet the Moomins:

- During the Christmas season, Moominworld allows visitors to meet their favorite Moomin characters, including Moomintroll, Snufkin, and Little My. The characters roam about the park in the snow, snapping photos and telling children about their winter adventures in Moominvalley.

Christmas-themed Activities:

- Moominworld provides a variety of Christmas-themed events to keep families delighted. Children can decorate Moominhouse for the holidays, and make Christmas cards, gingerbread biscuits, and snow sculptures. The park hosts unique Christmas storytelling events, in which the Moomins gather around a nice, warm fire to hear famous tales about this time of year.

Sledding and Snow Fun:

- Winter Park Moominworld promises a lot of fun in the snow: sliding down hills, having snowball battles, and creating snow castles with the Moomin. The park offers winter nature walks guided by routes through a snowy forest, where visitors may see some unusual creatures along the way.

Food and Treats Festive:

- And no visit to Moominworld is complete without trying some of the park's delectable Christmas sweets. Families may warm up with hot cocoa, indulge in traditional Finnish Christmas goodies, and try the famed Moomin pancakes with jam and whipped cream.

Family Accommodation in Naantali

Many families visiting Moominworld this Christmas choose Naantali as their home base, an appealing seaside town with a lovely harbor and a welcoming environment.

The Naantali Spa Hotel

Naantali Spa Hotel is one of the most popular family resorts, offering rest and festive activities. The hotel is carefully adorned for Christmas; you may relax with your family in spa treatments, refresh yourself in indoor swimming pools, or easily travel to Moominworld, which is just a ferry ride away.

In conclusion, Finland has a diverse range of family-friendly Christmas activities that capture the joy of the season in unique and fascinating ways.

PRACTICAL TRAVEL TIPS

A vacation to Finland, particularly in the winter, is a journey into the realm of magic; but, it also poses distinct problems and considerations that must be addressed. To ensure that your vacation goes smoothly, you need to be prepared for the cold, understand how to move around, and be aware of numerous travel restrictions and safety standards. Here is some practical travel advice to help you have a smooth and pleasurable winter journey in Finland.

Essential Tips for Winter Travel in Finland

Winter in Finland is an ethereal experience, and being prepared determines one's level of comfort and enjoyment of the Arctic paradise.

Know the Weather Conditions:

Finnish winters are notable for being extremely cold, especially in the north, such as Lapland. In some regions, like Rovaniemi or Levi, the temperature can drop to as low as -30°C. Helsinki and southern Finland experience milder weather, with temperatures ranging from -5°C to -15°C. Pay close attention to the daily weather prediction during your visit, since the weather can change quickly, especially in the Arctic Circle.

- **Shorter Days:** During the severe winter months, days are short and daylight hours are limited, particularly in the north. In regions like Rovaniemi, you will only have a few hours of daylight and may even experience a polar night, which occurs when the sun does not rise for several weeks. So, limiting daylight may have an impact on your plans to the point where certain alterations to scheduled activities are worthwhile.

Prepare for the Snow and Ice:

Finnish winters are also known for severe snowfall and ice conditions. Heavy rains can make walking or driving dangerous, especially if you're not used to it. Prepare ahead of time and take extra care when traveling. Traction cleats or ice grips on shoes are excellent purchases for safely walking down icy streets.

- **Icy Roads:** If you intend to rent a car and drive in Finland, be prepared for icy and snowy conditions. Winter tires are required between November and

March; in some regions, particularly in Lapland, studded tires are advised. Always check weather forecasts and drive cautiously on snow-covered roadways.

Come to Terms with the Darkness:

Winter days are extremely short, particularly in northern Finland. In fact, in regions above the Arctic Circle, such as Saariselkä, you may experience Kaamos, or Polar Night, in which the sun does not rise beyond the horizon for several days or weeks. Rather than seeing the darkness as a drawback, it may enhance the magic of your trip, particularly for Northern Lights hunting or cuddling up by the fire after a long day outside.

What to Bring Along

Packing for a winter trip to Finland requires consideration. Of course, Arctic conditions necessitate appropriate clothes and gear, but you also want to be comfortable, stylish, and functional. Here are the things you will need:

Layering is key

This is Finland's cold winter, and wearing numerous layers is the best way to stay warm. This way, you may adjust based on the temperature and intensity of the activity.

- **Base Layer:** Start with a moisture-wicking base layer that will draw sweat away from your skin. Merino wool or synthetic thermal shirts and bottoms are ideal for this purpose.

- **Midde Layer:** The middle layer should be insulating in nature, similar to a fleece or down jacket. This layer is designed to help retain body heat and keep you warm.

- **Outer Layer:** A parka or heavy winter coat is an example of an outer layer that is both windproof and waterproof. Choose jackets with hoods to protect your head and face from snow and wind.

- **Leggings and Pants:** Thermal leggings or long johns are ideal for wearing under your pants. If you plan to ski or snowboard, waterproof ski trousers are a good option.

Accessories and Footwear

When it's severely chilly outside, accessories make a big difference in keeping you warm. Do not leave out these important ones:

- **Hat/Beanie:** A wool or fleece-lined hat is required. Allow it to cover your ears, which are particularly vulnerable to frostbite.

- **Gloves or Mittens:** They should be well-insulated and waterproof. Mittens are typically warmer than gloves, but if your hands require dexterity, wear thermal gloves with linings.

- **Scarf or Neck Gaiter:** Wear a wool scarf to protect your neck and face from the bitter winds, or simply use a buff.

- **Thermal Socks:** Wool socks are required to keep your feet warm. Make sure you have extra pairs in case they get wet.

- **Winter boots** should be warm, waterproof, and have high traction. You'll need boots with sufficient insulation that can withstand temperatures below zero.

Other Essentials

Sunglasses: Because snow reflects sunlight, people should wear sunglasses to avoid snow blindness, especially if they plan to spend time outside.

Portable charger: Cold weather quickly depletes battery life. Pack a portable charger for your phone or camera.

Moisturizer and Lip Balm: The cold, dry air can be harsh on your skin. Keep your skin hydrated with an excellent moisturizer, and protect your lips with a high-quality lip balm.

Getting Around Finland

Finland has typically strong public transit, making it reasonably easy to travel around even during snowy winter weather. Whether you're visiting Lapland for a Christmas adventure or enjoying Helsinki's Christmas markets, there are various transportation options available.

Trains

VR operates the Finnish railway system, which is reliable and comfortable for travel between major cities. Trains run between Helsinki and cities such as Tampere, Turku, and Rovaniemi, making them popular with both inhabitants and tourists.

- **Night Trains:** If you're traveling to Lapland, taking an overnight train is a great alternative. The Santa Claus Express from Helsinki to Rovaniemi travels even further north and includes sleeping cabins, a restaurant car, and enough storage space for winter gear.

- **Purchasing Tickets:** Train tickets are available online at VR or at the stations. Children, students, and seniors frequently receive discounts on trains.

Buses

Long-distance buses run by companies such as Matkahuolto and OnniBus are especially useful for shorter trips or reaching smaller communities. Buses travel often, are pleasant, and might be slightly less expensive than trains.

- **Bus Routes:** Buses connect practically all Finnish cities, even the isolated areas of Lapland, and you may even travel to ski resorts such as Levi and Saariselkä.

- **Travel Passes:** If you plan on taking the bus regularly, consider purchasing a travel pass that allows you unlimited travel within a specific time frame.

Domestic Flights

Domestic flights are the fastest way to travel long distances, such as from Helsinki to Lapland. Finnair and Norra provide regular domestic flights to northern destinations including Rovaniemi, Ivalo, Kittilä, and Kuusamo.

- **Airports in Finland:** Finland's principal international airport is Helsinki (HEL). Domestic flights in Lapland will land at Rovaniemi (RVN), Kittilä (KTT), Ivalo (IVL), and Kuusamo (KAO). Please keep in mind that smaller airports have fewer services and shorter operation hours.

- **Baggage and Services:** Before flying, check with your airline to see if there are any baggage limits. Most airlines have a luggage policy in place, particularly for those traveling with sporting equipment such as skis or snowboards.

Visa Requirements and Entry Information

Finland is a member of the Schengen Area, therefore visa requirements are dictated by your country of origin. Below is information on how to enter Finland as a tourist.

EU Travelers

- **Visa-Free Travel:** If you are from an EU/EEA nation, no visa is required to enter Finland. This country accepts legitimate national ID cards or passports from these nations for entrance.

- **Duration of Stay:** EU residents can stay in Finland for an unlimited period, but they must register with the local authorities if their stay exceeds three consecutive months.

Non-EU Travelers

- **Schengen Visa:** Those who are not residents of the EU/Schengen Zone may be required to obtain a Schengen visa before entering Finland. A Schengen visa permits for up to 90 days of travel within the Schengen Area in any given 180-day period.

- **Entry Visa Exemptions:** Citizens of some countries, including the United States, Canada, Australia, and Japan, are permitted to enter Finland without a visa for 90 days out of every 180 days. However, all such visitors will be required to present a valid passport for admittance.

Entry Requirements:

Regardless of your nationality, you must demonstrate the following upon arrival at the Finnish border:

- A valid passport or national ID card, in the case of EU nationals.

- Proof of sufficient funds for your stay.

- Travel insurance protects you from any medical emergencies during your vacation.

Airport: Operating Hours, Baggage Allowances, and Services

Most Finnish airports are modern and functioning. Helsinki Airport is the main international airport, however, for flights to Lapland, the regional airports of Rovaniemi and Kittilä are equally good.

Helsinki Airport - HEL

- **Operating Hours:** The airport is open 24 hours a day. Many airport services run around the clock.

Restaurants and stores are fine, and saunas are accessible.

- **Baggage Allowances:** Check with your specific airline; baggage restrictions differ. Domestic flights tend to have fewer allowances, especially on low-cost carriers.

- **Services** include free Wi-Fi, luggage storage, and a selection of eateries. Helsinki Airport celebrates Christmas with decorations and special services, including gift wrapping.

Lapland Airports

- Lapland's main airports are **Rovaniemi RVN, Kittilä KTT, and Ivalo IVL,** which are smaller and have fewer operational hours than Helsinki-Vantaa Airport. Check in advance to see whether your flight will be late.

- **Christmas Season Traffic:** The Christmas season is quite congested at all of Lapland's airports. You may expect crowds, especially around December. –

Customs and Border Protection for Visitors

The country follows normal Schengen Area customs norms. Customs checks may be required upon entry into the nation depending on the mode of transportation you use and the nature of the items you are carrying.

Customs Declarations

- **EU Travelers:** If you are traveling from within the EU, there are no significant limits on what you can carry into Finland as long as it is for personal use.

- **Non-EU Travelers:** Travelers from outside the EU will face limits and tariffs on such items. For example, you can bring a certain amount of tobacco and alcohol duty-free.

- **Prohibited Items:** Certain substances are not permitted, including weapons, explosives, and narcotics. The full list of banned items can be seen on Finland's customs website.

Duty-Free Shopping

- **Travelers from Outside the EU:** If you live outside the EU, you can shop in Finland tax-free. During your stay in Finland, visit stores with the Tax-Free sign and request a tax-free form when making purchases. You can get your VAT refund when you leave the airport.

Health and Safety Concerns

Finland is a fairly safe country, however, there are several health and safety precautions you should take when going during the winter.

Winter Safety Tips and Dealing with the Cold

Finland's Arctic winters can be harsh, so it's important to be prepared.

- **Keep Warm:** Always wear appropriate winter clothes, especially if you plan to be outside for an extended amount of time. Avoid staying out for too long without taking breaks indoors.

- **Watch out for Frostbite:** Extremely cold temperatures can cause frostbite on exposed skin in a very short amount of time. Symptoms include skin turning white and numbness or tingling. If you feel these symptoms, immediately get indoors.

- **Stay Hydrated:** Cold air is dry, and it's easy to forget you're dehydrating. Drink plenty of water, even if you do not feel thirsty.

- **Slippery Surfaces:** Snow and ice make walking dangerous. Wear spiky grips in your shoes and tread gently on icy surfaces.

Emergency Contacts and Procedures

In the event of an emergency, you should know who to call. Finland's emergency system is highly efficient, and most services are available in English.

- **Emergency Numbers:** The Finnish general emergency number is 112, which connects to the police, fire department, ambulance, and other emergency agencies.

- **Medical Services:** The medical facilities in Finland are remarkable. If you become ill or injured, seek medical attention as soon as possible at a healthcare facility, terveysasema, or hospital. Apteekki pharmacies are adequately stocked with over-the-counter medications for minor injuries and illnesses.

- **Insurance:** If you intend to participate in any winter sport, such as skiing or snowmobiling, be sure you have travel insurance that covers medical emergencies.

Finland is a true winter wonderland for travelers, but it pays to be prepared for cold weather and unexpected events when traveling. The following pointers will help you prepare for whatever comes your way throughout the holiday season, from breathtaking, snow-covered landscapes to joyful Christmas markets.

LOCAL ETIQUETTE & CULTURAL TIPS FOR CHRISTMAS

Finland is well-known for its deep-rooted traditions of respect for nature and community. This is especially important during the Christmas season: whether you're seeing the cities, participating in festivities, or traveling to Lapland, understanding local etiquette and cultural norms can enrich your experience while not disrespecting Finnish life. In this section, we look at Finnish Christmas traditions, sauna culture, what not to do as a visitor, and how to respect Sami traditions while visiting Lapland.

Finnish Christmas Customs and Holiday Etiquette

Christmas in Finland is a magical blend of family, faith, and modern festivities. It is the time of year when Finns retire to their homes to enjoy nature and spend time with their loved ones. So, here are some important customs and etiquette tips to remember over the holidays.

Christmas Eve: The Heart of the Celebration

Christmas Eve, also known as Jouluaatto, is the most important day for most Finns. It is held on December 24th. While many countries still celebrate on Christmas Day, most Finnish Christmas customs take place on Christmas Eve.

- **Family Gatherings:** Christmas Eve is dedicated to the closest relatives. The families get together for a wonderful dinner, exchange gifts, and have a calm and contemplative evening. Please keep in mind that this is a highly private occasion, thus being invited to a Finnish household for Christmas Eve is significant.

- **Visiting Cemeteries:** Perhaps the most distinctively Finnish thing to do is to visit cemeteries on Christmas Eve and put candles on the graves of loved ones. The cemeteries are illuminated by candlelight, creating a serene and picturesque scene. If you want to participate in this tradition, be respectful and keep a calm, introspective demeanor.

- The **Declaration of Christmas Peace**, which dates back to the 1300s and is declared in places such as Turku, marks the start of Christmas with a call to everyone to engage in peace and goodness. This is a solemn occasion, so be calm and respectful if you attend.

Christmas and Boxing Day

- **Christmas Day:** December 25th (Joulupäivä) is a day of rest. Finns spend their afternoon at home relaxing after the previous evening's feasts and festivities. Many companies and shops will be closed, so if you plan to visit Finland on Christmas Day, you should stock up on supplies.

- **Boxing Day (Tapaninpäivä),** on December 26th, is a much more relaxed occasion. Traditionally, it was a day to connect with friends and family, but it is also becoming increasingly popular to participate in other outdoor sports such as skiing or ice skating.

Sauna Traditions at Christmas

The sauna is an integral part of Finnish culture, and this is especially true during the holiday season. In Finland, almost every household has a sauna, either in the home or shared by many apartment buildings. For many people, Christmas

Eve is incomplete without a visit to the sauna. Many people consider this a fundamental requirement.

Sauna on Christmas Eve

Many Finnish families begin the holiday season with a traditional sauna session to purify both body and mind. Here's how to experience the sauna like a local:

- **Timing:** It is typically consumed in the late afternoon on Christmas Eve, before the evening meal. It is a time for silence and introspection; avoid noisy conversations and interruptions.

- **Sauna Etiquette:** The sauna is intended for relaxation and quietness. It is customary to go naked in Finnish saunas, but if you are not comfortable, you can cover your body with a towel. It is critical to shower before entering the sauna room, and to be polite to others--do not monopolize the seats and allow others to splash water over the stones, known as löyly in Finnish.

- **Sauna with Santa:** This is a delight offered by certain hotels and cabins in Lapland, in which Santa Claus visits the sauna. This is one of the most entertaining variants of sauna use, and it is especially popular among youngsters.

Public Saunas and Christmas Saunas for Tourists

If you don't have access to a private sauna, many towns and cities provide public saunas where you can share this important Finnish tradition. During the Christmas season, several public saunas conduct special tourist sessions with festive decorations, traditional refreshments such as glögi (mulled wine), and sauna rituals.

- **Outdoor Ice Saunas:** In some regions, particularly in Lapland, you can enjoy an outdoor sauna before plunging into a cold lake. Not for the faint of heart, but it's an exhilarating way to experience Finnish winter.

Dos and Don'ts for Tourists during Finnish Winter Holidays

As a tourist, it is critical not to annoy locals with your unintentional faux pas during the Christmas holiday season in Finland. Anyway, here is the crucial do and don't list for Finland at Christmas:

Do: Enjoy the Silence

- The Finns are highly sensitive to stillness, especially during the holiday season. People should not be unduly noisy, whether in a public sauna, a Christmas market, or simply strolling through nature. In general, being loud or disruptive is considered impolite.

Don't: Simply Drop In

- If you are asked to a Finnish home for a Christmas supper or celebration, it is customary to notify the host in advance whether or not you will be able to attend. It might be impolite to just show up. Arrive on time and bring a modest gift, such as chocolates or a bottle of wine, to help round out the evening.

Do: Respect Nature

- Finland is a country known for its unspoiled natural beauty, and Finns values its natural heritage. When visiting Finnish national parks or forests, adhere to the Leave No Trace concept. Don't litter or disturb wildlife. In the winter, keep to marked pathways to avoid destroying vulnerable ecosystems.

Don't: Avoid using the sauna

- If you are requested to join others in a sauna, do not pass it up due to awkwardness. Of course, it is customary to go without clothes, but no one will judge you if you cover up with a towel. The sauna is intended to be a relaxing and uniting experience, and it is regarded as respectful to attend when invited.

Do: Learn a few Finnish phrases

- While most Finns speak great English, knowing a few Finnish words goes a long way toward gaining respect for the local culture. Basic greetings like "Hyvää joulua" (Merry Christmas) or "Kiitos" (Thank you) are much appreciated and go a long way towards connecting with the people.

Respecting Sami Traditions in Lapland

These are the indigenous of Lapland, and they take pleasure in a rich culture that is inextricably linked to the region's landscapes and traditions. Tourists who visit Lapland during Christmas should not miss out on honoring Sami taboos and traditions.

Understanding Sami Culture

For generations, the Sami have lived in northern Finland, Sweden, Norway, and Russia. Sámi Sápmi, in the northern section of Finnish Lapland, is home to the majority of Sami people. The culture is inextricably linked to reindeer herding, traditional crafts, and the natural world.

Respect the Sami Reindeer Herding Traditions

Reindeer herding is vital to Sami culture, and it is important to be respectful if you participate in activities such as reindeer sleigh rides or reindeer safaris. Always follow your guide's recommendations and avoid disturbing the animals.

- **Safaris with Reindeer:** When scheduling a reindeer safari, choose experiences offered by Sami-owned businesses. This would go a long way toward ensuring that tourism dollars reach the local community and that the experience is authentic and respectful of Sami customs.

Avoid Cultural Appropriation

Gákti is the Sami traditional clothing, which is worn on special occasions and at festivities. It is also critical to never wear or produce replica Sami clothes unless you have been encouraged to do so by a Sami. Wearing gákti as a costume is not appropriate.

Visit Sami Museums and Cultural Centers

To learn more about Saami culture, visit the Siida Sami Museum in Inari, which has exhibitions on Saami history and traditions, as well as Saami life now. The museum provides insight into how to live as a Saami and, in fact, connects with the earth.

Respectful Communication with Saami Elders

If you come across any Sami elders during your stay in Lapland, please treat them with respect. Elders are highly respected in Sami culture, and their knowledge of the land and traditions is invaluable. When they tell you anything or share a story, pay close attention and refrain from interfering.

Conclusion

Finnish Christmas traditions are a genuine expression of appreciation for family, nature, and the country's heritage. You'll get a lot more out of your trip and a better understanding of this distinct culture if you embrace local customs, respect Sami traditions, and take part in Finnish holiday rituals like saunas.

UNIQUE FINNISH CHRISTMAS FOODS AND DRINKS

Finnish Christmas is a time for festive decorations, snowy landscapes, sauna baths, and a culinary festival with rich flavors and traditional foods. Finnish Christmas food accurately reflects the northern environment, where hearty meals are cooked to keep people warm throughout the coldest months of the year. From traditional Christmas buffets to small cafes providing seasonal goodies, Finnish holiday cuisine is an integral element of the festive experience. From restaurants offering traditional favorites to home-cooked dinners, the Finnish Christmas table is a veritable feast of tastes that blend in savory, sweet, and warming foods in such a beautiful mix.

Must-Try Finnish Christmas Dishes

During the holidays, the Finns always have perennial favorites that never leave their tables, and the majority of the drinks have been passed down through generations. Traditional Finnish Christmas dishes use seasonal ingredients. Here's a list of some of the most iconic must-try Christmas meals in Finland.

1. Joulukinkku—Christmas Ham

The joulukinkku, or Christmas ham, is a traditional Finnish holiday dish. This delicate, oven-baked ham is drizzled with mustard and frequently topped with breadcrumbs for a golden finish. Joulukinkku is typically served hot or cold in thin slices, along with potatoes, casseroles, and pickled vegetables.

- **How to Enjoy:** Traditionally, Finnish families bake joulukinkku overnight, filling the house with warm, savory odors. The ham is served with mustard, usually Finnish-made sinappi, which is slightly sweet and acidic.

2. Laatikot (Christmas casseroles)

Laatikot, or traditional Christmas casseroles, are an essential part of each Finnish Christmas supper. During the holidays, you can discover three primary types of casseroles, each with its own flavor profile:

- **Porkkanalaatikko (Carrot Casserole):** Boiled and mashed carrots are combined with rice and a hint of nutmeg to create this delicious and nourishing casserole. It's ideal as a side dish with joulukinkku.

- **Lanttulaatikko,** also known as Swede or Rutabaga Casserole, is a dish similar to carrot casserole but made with mashed swede or rutabaga. It has a smooth and creamy texture with a little earthy flavor. It may be slightly more flavorful than the carrot variant.

- **Perunalaatikko,** sometimes known as Potato Casserole, is a simple but popular meal made with mashed potatoes that is sometimes sweetened with syrup. It is the least frequent of the three, yet it may still be seen on many Finnish family tables.

3. Rosolli (Finnish Beetroot Salad)

Rosolli is a vibrant Christmas meal that would brighten any Christmas table. This chilly meal consists of finely sliced beetroot, carrots, potatoes, and occasionally pickled herring. It is commonly served with sour cream or vinaigrette dressing. The vibrant pink color at the heart adds visual appeal to this meal, which matches its taste.

- **Cultural Tip:** Rosolli is a staple of the Finnish Christmas buffet, and it is typically served with a sour sauce consisting of whipped cream and vinegar. It's refreshing because it offsets the richness of the casseroles and ham.

4. Kalapöytä (Fish table)

Fish is a staple in Finnish cuisine, and various fish dishes can be seen on the Christmas table. The name kalapöytä refers to a variety of herring, salmon, and occasionally whitefish preparations.

- **Graavilohi: Cured Salmon -** A favorite appetizer or main meal cured in salt, sugar, and dill. Thinly sliced and frequently served with mustard-dill sauce on rye toast.

- **Silakka,** also known as pickled herring, is another popular Christmas delicacy in Finland. It is typically marinated in a sweet or sour sauce. These can be paired with mustard, onions, or other creamy sauces.

5. Joulutortut (Finnish Christmas Pastries)

Sweetly, Joulutortut is an absolute must-have for the holiday season. These star-shaped pastries are constructed from flaky puff pastry and filled with luumuhillo or prune jam. Powdered sugar is sometimes sprinkled over the pastry to add added sweetness. The star is both joyful and reminiscent of the Star of Bethlehem.

- **Where to find:** During the Christmas season, these joulutorttu are readily available in most bakeries, cafes, and supermarkets throughout Finland. They pair well with glögi, a Finnish variation of mulled wine.

6. Piparkakut (gingerbread cookies)

Piparkakut, or gingerbread cookies, are an essential part of any Finnish Christmas. These spicy and crunchy cookies, which are commonly shaped like stars, hearts, and snowflakes, are consumed throughout the festive season.

- **Making it Fun:** Baking and decorating gingerbread cookies is a tradition for many families. You can also try baking piparkakut during Finnish Christmas workshops and markets.

7. Riisipuuro (Rice porridge)

Christmas Eve morning traditionally begins with a calming bowl of riisipuuro, or rice porridge. A basic combination of rice, milk, and a sprinkle of salt, it is typically served with a dollop of luumukiisseli, prune soup, or cinnamon and sugar.

- **Fun Tradition:** An almond is hidden inside one of the riisipuuro dishes. Whoever discovers the almond is considered to have good fortune for the coming year!

Christmas Buffets and Traditional Holiday Meals

The Finnish Christmas buffet, or joulupöytä, is an essential aspect of the Christmas celebration. This festive supper is served on Christmas Eve and usually includes both cold and hot dishes. Here are some of the items you may find on a typical Finnish joulupöytä.

Cold Dishes

- **Kalapöytä** refers to a fish table, which, as previously stated, is extremely important to the buffet. Pickled herring, cured salmon, and smoked seafood can all be found there. These are typically eaten with black rye bread and sauces.

- **Cold Cuts:** In addition to fish, cold slices of smoked reindeer or ham are commonly served with pickled vegetables and condiments such as mustard.

Hot Dishes

- **Joulukinkku:** The main meal of the hot dishes is Christmas ham, which is always served with different types of laatikkoa and potatoes.

- **Sautéed reindeer** is a popular Christmas treat in some parts of Finland, particularly in Lapland. It is served with mashed potatoes and lingonberry sauce.

Desserts

- **Piparkakut:** Gingerbread cookies, like joulutorttu and other sweet pastries, are a fundamental component of desserts.

- **Glögi:** To wash it all down, many Finns drink a warm glass of glögi, a spicy mulled wine that is frequently served with almonds and raisins.

Best Restaurants and Cafés to Try Finnish Holiday Cuisine

At Christmas, great restaurants and quiet tiny cafes throughout Finland's cities and towns provide local traditional delicacies. Everything from a full-fledged lavish Christmas banquet to the coziest modest coffee shop serving pastries.

1. Savotta, Helsinki

Savotta, located in the middle of Helsinki, offers rustic and authentic Finnish cuisine. This restaurant specializes in traditional Finnish cuisine, including warm Christmas feasts with reindeer, fish, and festive casseroles. The décor is quite Finnish-forest-cabin-like, so expect a warm mood for this type of supper.

- **What to Try:** This Christmas dinner has reindeer filet, mushroom soup, and traditional Finnish Christmas treats.

2. Ravintola Kappeli (Helsinki)

If you're looking for a refined Christmas dinner experience, Kappeli in Helsinki has you covered. Esplanadi Park's historic restaurant elevates traditional Finnish holiday cuisine to a gourmet level.

- **What to Try:** Kapelli's famous Christmas buffet has graavilohi, pickled herring, and rich desserts like luumu torttu.

3. Restaurant Aino (Rovaniemi)

Restaurant Aino is one of the greatest places to eat authentic Lapland food while visiting Rovaniemi during the Christmas season. The cuisine includes a lot of local produce, like reindeer and Arctic char, as well as traditional Christmas fare during the holiday season.

- **What to Try:** In addition to reindeer feasts, Aino seasonal delicacies include smoked salmon, sautéed mushrooms, and cloudberry desserts.

4. Cafe Ekberg (Helsinki)

Café Ekberg is one of Helsinki's oldest establishments and the ideal place to taste Finnish Christmas desserts with coffee. This old café, founded in 1852, is well-known for its exquisite joulutorttu and other seasonal delicacies.

- **What to Try:** Not to be missed: Finnish coffee with Ekberg's famed Christmas dessert and piparkakut.

5. Saaga (Helsinki)

Restaurant Saaga provides Lapland cuisine to Helsinki. Saaga is known for its rustic decor, original food, and traditional Finnish Christmas feast. The Christmas cuisine includes traditional reindeer dishes, game meats, and a variety of laatikkoa.

- **What to Try:** The sautéed reindeer with lingonberry sauce is a must-try, and the Christmas desserts are very good.

6. Santa's Salmon Place (Rovaniemi)

This eatery is truly unique due to its location near the Arctic Circle. Santa's Fish Place offers grilled fish over an open fire.

This restaurant should be on your list for a relaxed yet memorable Christmas lunch in Rovaniemi.

- **What to Try:** All of their fire-grilled salmon is served with rye bread and dill sauce, which makes for a delicious meal. With a warm cup of glögi, you'll feel like you're already in the holiday spirit.

Conclusion

Finnish Christmas cuisine is a rich and wonderful trip through history and culture. Whether it's a massive buffet in the capital city of Helsinki, pastry in a small café, or homemade food in Lapland with friends, the foods served represent nothing but Finland's heart and soul. Finnish Christmas meals, with their savory meats, robust casseroles, sweet pastries, and spiced drinks, genuinely warm up the season and give visitors a true experience of Finnish hospitality.

CHRISTMAS ITINERARIES IN FINLAND

Finland offers it everything this Christmas season, from snow-covered expenses to jubilant Helsinki streets. Finland has something for everyone's taste, from tranquil snow-covered scenery to lively marketplaces and quiet cafes. Here are some sample programs of various lengths that will help make your Finnish Christmas holiday as memorable as possible, regardless of how long you stay in Finland.

3-Day Christmas Itinerary (Lapland Focus)

Day 1: Arrival in Rovaniemi, Santa Claus Village

Morning:

- Arrived in Rovaniemi, Finnish Lapland's capital and Santa Claus' hometown.

- Check into your lodging, which might be a glass igloo or a timber cabin to experience the Arctic.

- Visit Santa Claus Village, where you may visit Santa Claus, get postcards at the Post Office, and browse in the Christmas-themed stores.

Afternoon:

- Take a ride on a reindeer sleigh through the winter forest.

- Visit Santa Claus Village to witness the Arctic Circle, which is marked by a white line.

Evening:

- Attend a traditional Lappish supper at a nearby restaurant (taste reindeer, Arctic char, and cloudberry sweets).

- Keep an eye out for the Northern Lights, either from your lodging or during a guided trip.

Day 2: Arctic adventure in Lapland

Morning:

- Go on a snowmobile safari to see the untouched Arctic countryside. A few tours will also give you the opportunity to go ice fishing on frozen lakes.

- Pay a visit to the Sami reindeer farm to learn about the traditional Sami culture and way of life.

Afternoon:

- Relax in a comfortable Lappish café and warm yourself with some glögi-heated wine and piparkakut-gingerbread cookies.

- Visit the Arktikum Science Museum to discover more about the Arctic's natural and cultural history.

Evening:

- Join an Aurora Hunting Tour by Sleigh or from the comfort of the Aurora Dome, where you can observe the Northern Lights through the clear roof.

Day 3: Winter Sports and Departure

Morning:

- Ski or snowboard at the Levi Ski Resort, or simply enjoy the panoramic views from a picturesque gondola ride.

- Alternatively, take a husky sledding tour of the snow-covered trails.

Afternoon:

- Get warm in a typical Finnish sauna.

- Before leaving for the airport, make a quick stop at the Rovaniemi Christmas Market to get any last-minute gifts.

5-Day Christmas Itinerary (Helsinki and Lapland Combo)

Day 1: Arrival in Helsinki, Christmas Charm in the Capital

Morning:

- When you arrive in Helsinki, check into your hotel and proceed right to Senate Square for the Helsinki

Christmas Market. Over 100 stalls sell crafts, presents, and wonderful seasonal delicacies.

Afternoon:

- Take a stroll from the Esplanadi to the city's main streets, which are brightly lit with Christmas lights and street entertainers filling the region with vitality.

- One of the attractions of a visit to Helsinki will undoubtedly be the Helsinki Cathedral, which is always beautifully illuminated throughout the Christmas season.

Evening:

- Dine at Savotta, a classic Finnish restaurant offering Lappish food in the heart of Helsinki.

- Listen to a Christmas concert at one of Helsinki's many lovely historic churches, such as the Uspenski Cathedral or the Temppeliaukio Rock Church.

Day 2: Helsinki's Markets, Design, and Culture

Morning:

- Begin by not missing Stockmann's Christmas Window Display, which exudes festive charm.

- Local Finnish boutiques provide handicrafts and Finnish design items such as Marimekko or Iittala.

Afternoon:

- Take a stroll through the Helsinki Design District for some independent shopping and art gallery browsing.

- Warm up with Finnish coffee, joulutortut, or Christmas sweets at Café Ekberg, one of Helsinki's oldest cafes.

Evening:

- Enjoy a Christmas sauna in Löyly, a sophisticated seaside sauna complex, and relax like the traditional Finns.

Day 3: Excursion to Rovaniemi, the Land of Winter Wonderland

Morning:

- Take the aircraft from Helsinki to Rovaniemi. It's only a 1.5-hour flight.

- Check in to a glass igloo or a cozy cottage.

Afternoon:

- Visit SantaPark, an indoor playground filled with holiday fun. Participate in Elf School, cookie decorating, and perhaps meet Mrs. Claus.

Evening:

- Dine at Santa's Salmon Place for delicious fire-grilled salmon served in a rustic atmosphere.

- Go on an Aurora Borealis expedition by sleigh, snowmobile, or reindeer.

Day 4: Lapland Adventures: Huskies, Snow, and Saunas

Morning:

- Take a husky safari, driving through the icy landscapes with friendly huskies leading the way.

Afternoon:

- Take a reindeer sleigh ride and visit a Sami cultural center to learn about the traditions of the local indigenous people.

- Enjoy a typical Finnish Christmas brunch in a Lappish restaurant.

Evening:

- Enjoy a private Arctic sauna under the stars. Perhaps see the Northern Lights again.

Day 5: Departure to Rovaniemi

Morning:

- Take a final wander around the Rovaniemi Christmas Market before heading to the airport.

7-Day Christmas Itinerary in Finland (Complete Holiday Experience)

Day 1: Arrival in Helsinki – Festivities in the Capital

Morning:

- Arrive in Helsinki and check in to your hotel.

- Take an early morning tour of Senate Square to admire the Giant Christmas Tree and its lights.

Afternoon:

- Visit the Helsinki Christmas Market to sample Finnish Christmas specialties such as riisipuuro and buy handmade crafts.

Evening:

- Have dinner at Kappeli, a renowned restaurant near Esplanadi Park.

Day 2: Helsinki: Markets, Museums, and Moomins

Morning:

- Continue your exploration of Helsinki's Christmas magic by visiting Stockmann's famed Christmas Window Display and the Old Market Hall, where you may sample Finnish specialties.

Afternoon:

- Visit the Moomin Museum for a fantastic experience, especially if you have children with you.

- Take a stroll along the pleasant and broadly enlightened Esplanadi Boulevard, stopping at local shops and boutiques. Evening: Christmas concert at the Helsinki Music Centre or Temppeliaukio Church.

Day 3: Porvoo & Coastal Christmas Markets

Morning:

- Take a day trip to Porvoo, a charming medieval village about an hour from Helsinki. Stroll through the Porvoo Christmas Market to find seasonal items and admire the magnificent ancient town.

Afternoon:

- Treat yourself to a nice drink at a neighborhood café before seeing the Porvoo Cathedral.

Evening:

- Return to Helsinki for dinner and, if possible, spend the evening outside with a visit to Löyly Sauna.

Day 4: Lapland's Rovaniemi and Santa Claus Village

Morning:

- Fly to Rovaniemi and settle into your warm winter accommodations.

- Head to Santa Claus Village for a full day of holiday fun, which includes meeting Santa, crossing the Arctic Circle, and visiting Christmas-themed attractions.

Evening:

- Enjoy dinner at Santa's Salmon Place, a one-of-a-kind Arctic dining experience.

- Join a guided snowmobile or reindeer journey to look for Aurora.

Day 5: Arctic Adventure in Levi

Morning:

- Proceed to Levi Ski Resort to ski or snowboard, or to ride the cable car and enjoy the winter wonderland scenery.

Afternoon:

- Visit the Levi Christmas markets and eat lunch in the village.

- Explore the forests on a snowshoeing excursion.

Evening:

- Take a traditional Finnish Christmas sauna in a snowy cabin.

Day 6: Reindeer Safaris and Sami Culture

Morning:

- Visit a Sami farm with reindeer and learn about traditional reindeer herding. Take a reindeer sleigh ride through the snow-covered terrain.

Afternoon:

- Savor a filling Lappish lunch that includes dishes like creamy potato casseroles and sautéed reindeer.

- Learn about the history and culture of the Arctic by visiting the Arktikum Museum in Rovaniemi..

Evening:

- Join another Northern Lights Tour, this time from the comfort of a heated Aurora Dome.

Day 7: Departure from Rovaniemi

Morning:

- Spend your last day at the Rovaniemi Christmas Market doing last-minute shopping before heading home.

Conclusion

These itineraries provide a comprehensive package of Christmas charm, from the capital city's festive markets to the snowy area of Lapland. Whether you have a few days or a whole week, you'll experience the touching charm and time-honored traditions of a Finnish Christmas.

FREQUENTLY ASKED QUESTIONS ABOUT CELEBRATING CHRISTMAS IN FINLAND

1. When should I travel to Finland for Christmas?

Christmas festivities in Finland take place between late November and early January. The festival's peak month is usually December. There is plenty of snow at that time, which adds to the winter wonderland atmosphere.

2. Where exactly is Santa Claus Village located?

Santa Claus' official hometown is Rovaniemi, where you can visit him at Santa Claus Village. Aside from his studio, the village also has a post office and other attractions for people of all ages.

3. What are some of the typical Finnish Christmas foods?

Rosolli, a beetroot salad, joulukinkku, ham, lipeäkala, dried fish, and a variety of pastries such as piparkakut, gingerbread cookies, and joulutorttu, tarts, are traditional Finnish Christmas dishes.

4. Are there any Christmas markets in Finland?

Yes, several bigger towns in Finland, including Helsinki, Turku, and Tampere, host Christmas markets. There are numerous kiosks selling handicrafts and food, including seasonal sweets, that add to the Christmas spirit.

5. How can I view the Northern Lights in Finland?

The Northern Lights are visible across Finland, particularly in Lapland. The most well-known places are Rovaniemi, Levi, and Saariselkä. Most of the time, this is done in tandem with snowmobiles or reindeer sleighs.

6. What kinds of activities may Finnish families engage in over the Christmas season?

During this period, families can have fun by visiting Santa Claus Village, making a snow castle, attending elf school, ice fishing, and trekking on winter trails. Most ski resorts are also very family-friendly.

7. Is it freezing in Finland over Christmas?

Yes, it can be very chilly in Finland over the Christmas season, with temperatures frequently dropping below freezing. It is critical to dress warmly in numerous layers, including thermal jackets, caps, gloves, and waterproof boots.

8. What are Finland's Distinctive Christmas Traditions?

Other unique Christmas customs in Finland include enjoying a Christmas sauna with your family and lighting candles in memory of loved ones who have passed away. Attending the Declaration of Christmas Peace in Turku is also an important component of most Finns' holiday celebrations.

9. What transportation choices are there for going around during the holidays in Finland?

Domestic aircraft, railroads, and buses connect major cities and regions. Of course, renting a car for travel is an option, especially if you wish to see more remote areas of the country. In any case, public transit in Finland is generally reliable and functional.

10. Do I need a visa to visit Finland over Christmas?

Visa requirements differ based on your nationality. Shorter visits do not require a visa if you are from the EU, Schengen Area nations, or some other countries. Other passengers may see the Finnish embassy website for entrance requirements.

11. What should I Pack for Christmas in Finland?

Pack Arctic-appropriate clothes such as thermal layers, insulated jackets, waterproof boots, caps, gloves, and scarves. Don't forget to bring a camera to capture the stunning winter landscapes and joyful moments!

12. What events or festivals does Finland celebrate during the Christmas season?

Yes, Christmas events take place all around Finland, including Christmas concerts, candlelight ceremonies, and local festivals that celebrate traditional practices. Events like the Helsinki Christmas Market and the Turku Christmas Peace Declaration fall into this category.

13. Where can I see Santa's reindeer in Finland?

Yes! Visitors to Lapland can visit and engage with reindeer on various farms. Many of these farms provide activities such as reindeer sleigh rides, allowing visitors to fully immerse themselves in this iconic Finnish tradition.

14. Can you stay in an ice hotel during Christmas?

Yes, Finland does have some ice hotels, like the Levi Ice Hotel and Kemi's SnowCastle. You will be able to remain in an unusually built room entirely made of ice and snow, with thermal sleeping bags for warmth.

15. What local crafts or gifts should I search for at the Finnish Christmas markets?

Local handicrafts sold at Finnish Christmas markets include handcrafted ornaments, wooden toys, and woolen clothing, among other things. Glass art and pottery are further examples of traditional Finnish craftsmanship. Cloudberry jam and Finnish chocolate are examples of unique foods that make excellent gifts.

CONCLUSION

A Christmas holiday in Finland is more than just a trip; it's a heartfelt experience with memories that will endure forever. Whether strolling through Helsinki's charming Christmas markets, witnessing the Northern Lights in Lapland, or enjoying traditional Finnish holiday delicacies in cozy restaurants, countless magical moments make the holiday season memorable in this country.

Experiences range from the vibrant city of Helsinki to the silent, snowy woodlands of Lapland, ensuring that every traveler—alone, with family, or on a romantic getaway—finds something to treasure. Children will be delighted to meet Santa Claus in his official village, while adventurers can thrill to reindeer sledding, snowmobiling, and ice fishing. Families will cherish building snow castles, attending elf schools, and visiting snow-covered national parks.

One of the unique features of a Finnish Christmas is its connection to the country's rich traditions. Finns cherish the holiday season, not only for the festivities but also for its quiet appreciation of nature and simple pleasures. From the Christmas sauna ritual to lighting candles in homes and churches, Finland's traditions warm the winter cold. Understanding and respecting local customs, like the Sami traditions in Lapland, will deepen your connection to Finnish culture and landscape, making your stay even more meaningful.

Practical recommendations on how to navigate winter, what to pack, and the best ways to explore the nation will ensure a smooth and enjoyable journey. This guide aims to provide you with all the information you need for a seamless, stress-free Finnish Christmas filled with beautiful moments.

Wherever you go in Finland this holiday season, you'll find a Christmas that is simple, warm, and timeless. Prepare to fall in love with this winter wonderland; the beauty of the season and the kindness of the people will stay with you forever. Travel safely and enjoy a fantastic Finnish Christmas.

Printed in Great Britain
by Amazon